Averroes

Averroes

A Rationalist in Islam

ROGER ARNALDEZ

Translated by
DAVID STREIGHT

UNIVERSITY OF NOTRE DAME PRESS
Notre Dame, Indiana

English Language Edition Copyright © 2000
University of Notre Dame Press
Notre Dame, Indiana 46556
All Rights Reserved
http://www.undpress.nd.edu

Manufactured in the United States of America

Translated by David Streight from the French *Averroès, un rationaliste en Islam* by Roger Arnaldez, published by Éditions Balland, 33, rue Saint-André-des-Arts, 75006 Paris (2d edition, 1998).

The publisher is grateful to
THE FRENCH MINISTRY OF CULTURE–CENTRE NATIONAL DE LIVRE
for support of the costs of translation.

© Éditions Balland, 1998

Library of Congress Cataloging-in-Publication Data
Arnaldez, Roger.
  [Averroès. English]
  Averroes : a rationalist in Islam / by Roger Arnaldez; translation by David Streight.
     p. cm.
  Includes bibliographical references and index.
  ISBN 0-268-02007-8 (cloth : alk. paper) — ISBN 0-268-02008-6 (pbk. : alk.paper)
  1. Philosophy, Islamic. I. Title.
B749.Z7 A6913 2000
181'.92—dc21   00-055196

∞ *This book is printed on acid-free paper.*

"Is it not time to raise the banner of Averroes (Ibn Rushd) and to carry it forward? Is it not time to say that, in our own era, his ideas suit everyone, the beggar as well as the prince?"

SALMAN RUSHDIE

Le Monde, 16 October 1997

Contents

INTRODUCTION
Judge, Physician, and Philosopher 1

CHAPTER I
Jurist 16

CHAPTER II
Physician 26

CHAPTER III
Commentator on Aristotle 31

CHAPTER IV
Philosopher and Theologian 79

CONCLUSION
A Personal Muslim Thinker 119

Chronology 129
Glossary 131
Bibliography 147
Annotated Index of Proper Names 149
About the Author 157

INTRODUCTION

Judge, Physician, and Philosopher

All religious thought is confronted with the problem of the relationship between reason and faith. The question ultimately arises: Is there not some realm of Being that cannot be explored by reason, a realm that both demands and justifies reliance on a faculty completely distinct from reason, a kind of intuition with direct access to a truth unreachable by the methods of rational research? This question suggests the existence of a world of suprasensible realities; it reduces reason to a faculty whose sole purpose is to turn sensory data into scientific knowledge. Reason cannot go beyond that knowledge; that is, it can never go beyond the world of perception and representation. Religious thought leaves it to philosophers to research and explain the nature of the relationship between the spiritual universe and the material universe, between the One and the many, between being and becoming, between the eternal and the temporal. And, because it is religious thought, it concerns itself with only the first—the spiritual—universe.

Religious thought can also reflect on the certitude that is the goal of all true knowledge, a certitude that is solidly established and protected from doubt of any kind. Is there only one real certitude, that based on reason? Or, does another certitude exist, that of faith? Abū Hamīd al-Ghazālī wrote in his *Al-Munqidh min al-Dalāl* ("The Book of Freedom from Error"): "It appeared to me that *certain* knowledge is that knowledge in which what is known unveils itself in such a way that no doubt remains, and to which no possibility of error or illusion may be attached." Ghazālī proceeds to examine sensory illusions that are swept aside by reason. In so doing, he imagines what reply the senses might give to the soul convinced by the arguments of reason which is passing judgment on the senses. Sensation says, "With what do you temper your confidence in rational things—for it is like the confidence you formerly had in sensory things, when you had true confidence in me? Without the judgment of reason, you would have continued to believe in me. Beyond the grasp of reason, however, perhaps there is another judge whose sentence would show the falsity of reason, just as the sentence of reason made the falsity of the senses manifest." For Ghazālī, this faculty superior to reason does in fact exist. It is, he believes, the faculty of delicious experience, the "taste" of the mystics. In this sense, religious thought turns toward an illuminative knowledge found also among philosophers who were inspired by Avicenna. There is a light that illuminates human thought from above and that comes from God, for it is written in the Qurʾān (24:35): "God is the light of heaven and earth." Revelation is also the product of this light.

Averroes, however, was not a religious thinker, and the problem of the relationship between faith and reason did not occur to him in terms like those we have just considered. It would be a serious error to believe that he was obliged to confront this problem because he played the dual role of a judge who had to apply Muslim Law* based on the Qurʾān, and of a commentator on Aristotle who was seduced by the Stagirite's thinking. For Averroes, cadi (a judge appointed by virtue of his superior knowledge of Islamic law) in Seville, and later Grand Cadi of Cordoba, the Law existed—it had been revealed—as every Muslim believes. In his eyes, however, this Law was rational, and we shall soon see in what sense this was true. For Averroes, a philosopher, this rationality is sufficient to make the Law obliga-

---

*Later written "the Law," to distinguish Islamic Law, of divine essence in the eyes of Muslims, from the law or laws made by men (ed. note).

tory; but for the common man, subject to the passions, another guarantee and another authority are needed. These are supplied by the Qurʾān, with its promises and its threats, with the rewards and punishments of an all-powerful and omniscient God, Whom not one of man's actions escapes.

The function of a judge is to know the difference between obedience and disobedience to the Law; it is not, in the name of reason, to convince the person who is judged by demonstrating that he has acted well or poorly, or that he had been just or unjust. It is thus in the name of the Law that the judge condemns, not in the name of reason. It is simply a matter of making sure, through oaths and witnesses, that such and such an action really did take place.

What we are seeing here is the essence of an idea that guided Averroes' attitude toward anything that pertained to religion, properly speaking. If there is a revealed religious truth, it is necessarily in complete accord with rational truth.

Now there is one more aspect of religion that is not really oriented toward philosophical truth, but rather, it might be said, toward the truth of common men insofar as they are not philosophers. Religion has a human side to it, in the sense that it takes human weaknesses into account. The Qurʾān recognizes this explicitly: in a time of need, man cries out to God; when the torment has passed, he forgets (*cf.* 1:12, 39:8 and 49); man is greatly unjust (14:34, 33:72), impulsive (17:11), fickle (70:19), rebellious (96:16), a hair-splitter and a squabbler (18:54, 36:77). The man who in no way resembles the sage must be constantly put on guard; this is one of the essential functions of Messenger-Prophets (cf. 71:1, 74:2). These human characteristics alone justify the necessity for a Revelation of the Law. That being said, let us note that Averroes, unlike such philosophers as Fārābī, Miskawayh, and Avicenna, does not ask himself what prophetic knowledge consists of, how the prophet receives such knowledge, and *a fortiori* if such knowledge is even possible. On the other hand, he is critical of philosophers who attempt to integrate revealed concepts into philosophical learning, and then extract from this integration truths or an order of truths that might explain both the being of the universe in its entirety or in its parts, and the place of man in this universe. This way of proceeding is what Averroes condemns under the name of dialectics.

Averroes' thought presents an irrefutable unity, even if he, as both philosopher and commentator on Aristotle, may have had differing opinions on some of the finer points of the Stagirite's work (particularly with regard to the thorny question of the intellect). In such cases, he is always careful to explain the reasons for his hesitations. Whatever the situation, we shall see that he was indelibly marked by the logical methodology of the Greek thinker who was commonly known, in Arabic, as the "Master of Logic" (*sahib al-mantiq*). But he was not unaware of the fact that application of this method is not something that happens all by itself, and that it does occasionally leave one with problems that are not perfectly explained. These are not, however, reasons to give up the method, in order to look for other paths to solutions that could end up being purely imaginary or plausible, but fallacious. Although Averroes was a dedicated disciple of Aristotle, he did not think that the master's work was complete and definitive. What was definitive was the path that he laid out and the truths that he was able to establish firmly by following this path. Moreover, philosophical thought did not stop with Aristotle: Averroes believed in the proges of knowledge from one generation to another, and from this point of view, he could claim kinship with an important passage in the *Metaphysics* (α, 993b15 . . .), about which he said: "The Ancients, with respect to the Moderns, hold the same place as do fathers with respect to their sons, except that the generative act of the Ancients is nobler than that of fathers [. . .] and imitation of them is more just." If Aristotle owed thanks to his predecessors, despite the little knowledge of reality they had, how much more should we thank Aristotle himself, for all the wisdom he bequeathed to his successors! "And the thanks that is owed him in particular consists in keeping his teachings carefully, writing commentaries on them, and explaining them to all men. Actually, the *law* that is particular to philosophers is that of examining closely the totality of beings, because there is no nobler way to worship the Creator than by knowing His works." This appeal to God and His creation, like the idea of a law particular to philosophers that Averroes expresses by the religious word *sharīʿa*, does not have a religious character, but both show that the domain of the search for truth, that of divine creation, has a breadth that far exceeds the realm that Aristotle was able to explore.

But is there a unity—an interior unity—to the life of Averroes, the judge, the doctor, the philosopher? A number of Western historians have felt that he was a man with two faces, one a believer, and the other a skeptic, perhaps even an atheist. According to this theory, Averroes *appeared* to capitulate to the outward constraints of the religious community that condemned renegades and threatened them with a punishment that could be as severe as death. But we shall see that this is in no way true. The facts weigh against such an interpretation, for it turns the philosopher into a theorist of the doctrine of double truths. In reality, one cannot separate the Muslim who applied the Law from the thinker who commented on Aristotle and believed in the truth of his thought. God alone knows the depth of hearts, it is said. But since the heart has its reasons, it is not impossible to see into them. Let us not forget that man is, for both Averroes and Aristotle, a "political animal." It was thus normal for the Cordoban philosopher to be interested in man, hence in himself, in the light of this definition. Averroes took into consideration Plato's politics, part of which he wrote a commentary on. He could not help but think of himself as a member of a community whose nature and demands are studied by philosophy. We shall attempt to examine Averroes' life and work across all his different activities, without shattering the unity of his personality.

Life and Education

Averroes, whose complete name was Abū'l-Walīd Muhammad ibn Ahmad Muhammad ibn Rushd, was born in Cordoba in 520/1126. Since the year 500/1106, a great part of southern Spain had been under the rule of the Almoravid emir ʿAlī ibn

Yūsuf ibn Tāshufīn, who died in 537/1143. The emir had devoted his life, quite successfully, to the struggle against the Christians, but he had had to restrain the ambitions of a number of the members of his family. Confronted by seditious movements stirred up by intertribal quarrels, he never had managed to consolidate the political edifice left by his father Yūsuf. In addition, he had been forced to deal with the dangers caused by the uprising provoked by the preaching of Ibn Tūmart. He promoted a rigid doctrine of the unity of God, called the *tawhīd*, a word which gave rise to the name for the Almohad (*al-muwahhidūn*) Dynasty. But despite this critical situation ʿAlī ibn Yūsuf's reign coincided with one of the most brilliant periods in the history of the Muslim West, in the Maghreb and in Spain. The sovereign was surrounded by men of letters. Cordoba once again became an intellectual capital, a meeting place for poets and the learned. It was in this milieu that the young Averroes received his early education.

On the other hand, the country at that time was under the control of particularly intransigent jurists of the Mālikī school. It was they who had condemned to be burned al-Ghazālī's important work *Rebirth of the Sciences of Religion* (*Ihyaʾ ʿulūm al-Din*). We might wonder why they attacked a work whose religious significance was beyond question. The reason is simple: al-Ghazālī had spoken out against their school. The history of the Mālikī school is complex. In the beginning, the Mālikī school claimed to base law on Medinan tradition. The reason was evident: since Medina was the city of the Prophet, it was there that the practice of the Law was guaranteed by the very example of the Messenger of God. We will not go into the polemics concerning the rite of Mālik; rather, we will limit ourselves to pointing out that in North Africa the Mālikī school was known for the particular interest it showed in applications of the law (*furūʿ*) to the detriment of principles (*usūl*); personal effort (*ijtihād*) in interpreting the Qurʾān and the *hadith* was abandoned in favor of manuals. It is clear that relying on applications of the Law opened the door to control over every aspect of a person's life, and to a veritable inquisition. Ghazālī decried this alteration of the nature of the Law, showing that the rite of Mālik, thus applied, no longer had any connection to the true spirit of religious law. The Almoravids encouraged the study of the treatises of *furūʿ*. But Ibn Tūmart declared war against them, and thus stood in opposition to the importance that jurists of the Mālikī school had assumed in political life.

The Mahdī Ibn Tūmart, whose government and thought were so influential in Muslim Spain, died in 523/1130, shortly after Averroes' birth. His successor, ʿAbd al-Muʾmin, who came from an Islamicized Berber tribe, was proclaimed in 527/1132. Together, the two inaugurated the reformist movement that characterized the Almohad era, during which Averroes' different activites blossomed.

Averroes belonged to an important Spanish family. Biographies provide us with information that only goes back to his grandfather's generation. However, a manuscript in the Escorial contains a treatise of clinical medicine from the 11th century whose author says he took care of one of his friends, named Ibn Abī Rushd, who could have been an ancestor of Averroes. In any case, his father was cadi; his grandfather, who died in 520/1126, and who was cadi and imam in the Great Mosque of Cordoba, was a famous juridical consultant of the Mālikī school who left a book on law entitled *Premises* (al-Muqaddamāt) *aimed at facilitating the explanation of the demands made by the qualifications of the code* (al-mudawwana) *relative to legal sentences and solid legal traditions for the purpose of explaining the principal questions that are problematical.* This long title sums up the work's goals and serves as a reminder of the polemics that the rite of Mālik engendered. It was a question, on the one hand, of defining exactly which human actions were to be judged, and on the other, of determining which traditions (especially which Medinese traditions) were admissible as authentic, so that differences of opinion between jurists (especially those of the Mālikī school) could be avoided and a consensus (*ijmāʿ*) realized. The book aimed at enlightening the readers of the *Mudawwana*, Saḥnūn's great treatise that had established the Mālikī school as a strict school of law in North Africa. It would have been impossible for Averroes not to know his grandfather's work, although there clearly was no direct influence, since he died the same year that Averroes was born.

Although he claimed to belong to the Mālikī school, whose weight and rigidity in the Almoravid community has already been pointed out, the author of the *Muqaddamāt* appears to have been open-minded and relatively liberal, for his time, and we may assume that these attitudes were passed on to his family. In fact, he intervened to have the philosopher Avempace (Ibn Bājja) freed from prison, where, accused of heresy, he had been sent by the Almoravid Ibrāhīm ibn Yusūf ibn Tāshfīn. In any case, in contrast to many western adherents to the Mālikī school, who turned away from the study of "principles of law" drawn from examination of the Qurʾān and the Prophetic Tradition, he recommended researching proofs according to a logically coherent method. At the beginning of his book he wrote: "Divine Laws can be studied thoroughly only if one knows the obligation they impose, and the only path to knowing their obligation passes either through knowledge of God according to the attributes of essence and actions that belong to Him, or through the signs of proof that take the place of knowledge [. . .]. God is known only through speculation regarding the signs of proof that He has made available in order that He might be known and that they might be used as proof. But only he who has reason capable of speculating and proving is able to speculate and carry out the proof." His grandson would never say anything fundamentally different. God gave man the faculty of intellectual thought, and in the Qurʾān He ceaselessly urges him to make use of it, by recalling all the signs (*āyāt*) that He placed in the world for people capable of intellectual thought (*li-qawm^{in} yaʿqilūn*, 2:164). Averroes, as shall be seen, relied on revealed texts of this kind, not to justify a speculative theology (*kalām*), but, like his grandfather, to authorize the use of a rational method in the juridical search for the principles of what the laws require of men. We will encounter this question again in the chapter on Averroes the jurist.

We should not think that the young Averroes' education was limited to those disciplines in which he would later specialize and become renowned. First of all, in his Muslim society he certainly would have been instructed in theology. We know that he studied the Ashʿarite *kalām*. This school of thought was characterized by its teaching with regard to the happy medium, in belief, between rational theology and purely literalist theology. This happy medium is difficult to find. Let us go back to what Ghazālī said in his book on the subject. Some men, he says, believe in God and in the veracity of His Messenger; they follow his law in their worship and in their actions. "They must be left in their present state." They have no need for theology. God does not ask that people believe out of rational certainty. On the other hand, there are those who lean toward the infidels and the innovators: "They are of weak intelligence, hardened in an imitation they have followed from childhood into adulthood; only the whip and the sword are useful for them." Others believe from imitation and hearsay, "but they have no lack of wisdom or penetration, with the result that they experience problems elicited by doubts they hold regarding their beliefs." Their interior peace is shaken: "They must be treated gently to enable them to regain their peace and to thrust aside their doubts by appropriate words that they can hear." It might be enough to read them a verse from the Qurʾān, to report a hadith, or to pass on something said by someone they esteem. Often, that suffices; "if not, it is permissible to cure them with a clear proof, but only to the extent that is necessary and with a proof that pertains to the point of difficulty." There are, finally, men who hold fast to error in whom signs of intelligence and wisdom are noticeable. We can expect that they will recognize what in reality the doubts or tendencies to doubt that assail them are. "Those men must be drawn to truth with gentleness, they must be pointed in the direction of the true beliefs, not by an array of argumentation and intolerant doctrines, for such a procedure increases the causes of error and incites people to persevere and be stubborn in straying." We thus see that speculative theology, in its dogmatic form, is more dangerous than it is useful. The happy medium therefore is found in a reasonable reflection that lies at the level of texts and that does not claim to explain them with reasons that are foreign to them, or to pull from them what they are not saying. In this form, Ashʿarism could be accepted by Averroes. For him, a theology that claims to confront innovators and refute them has no persuasive value; that is what he criticizes in the—albeit quite modest—Muʿtazilism that he rejects as dialectical thought.

Averroes received an excellent juridical education. He knew by heart the imam Mālik's *Muwattaʾ*, a fundamental work for Malikism. His teacher was al-Hāfiz Abū Muhammad ibn Rizq, and he became very competent in his knowledge of *khilāf,* the science of controversies and differences of opinion in legal matters. One of his biographers also says he spent a short time studying with Ibn Bashkuwāl, who had been his grandfather's auditor in Seville. He was an erudite man endowed with an astounding memory and dedicated to teaching; he was considered to be the last of the Cordoban traditionists. In this case, Averroes would have been initiated into the science of the transmission of traditions, which is in no way unlikely, although he mainly devoted his attention to the science of "principles" (*usūl*), as we shall shortly see.

In medicine, Averroes' teacher was Abū Jaʿfar ibn Hārūn al-Tarjālī, who lived in Seville, and to whom Ibn Abī Usaybiʿa devoted a few lines in his book on the classes of doctors: "He was among the most important inhabitants of Seville, an accomplished philosopher, established in this field, passionate about the works of Aristotle and the other early philosophers, excellent and distinguished in the art of medicine, experienced in its foundations and applications, a good pracitioner in the treatment of the ill, praiseworthy in the application of his methods." The story is told of a child who had a splinter in his pupil, and was in desperate need of attention. The father took the child to be examined by Abū Jaʿfar and promised him 300 dinars if he save the child's eye. Abū Jaʿfar responded that he did not need the money; he would care for the child, and save the eye if God were willing. Then he proceeded to treat the child with the result that his eye was saved. Abu Abī Usaybiʿa informs us that the doctor was in the service of Abū Yaʿqūb (the Almohad caliph who ruled from 558/1163 to 580/1184, about whom we shall speak later). Moreover, Abū Jaʿfar was the pupil, in Seville, of the traditionist jurist Abū Bakr ibn al-ʿArabī, and studied *hadith* under his direction. The personality of this learned encyclopedist, whose teaching certainly left its mark on Averroes, helps us to understand the intellectual milieu—open to knowledge from a wide array of fields—in which Averroes grew up, and to which he owed his own vast culture.

As has been seen, the Mālikī jurists had condemned Ghazālī's theology, but it is probable, nevertheless, that Averroes came into contact with some of his works during the course of his early education, long before he came to criticize his book against the philosophers, the *Tahāhut al-falāsifa* ("The Downfall of the Philosophers"). The jurist Abū Bakr ibn al-ʿArabī, who returned from the East in 493/1100, had actually been cadi in Seville, and had taught there; he had met Ghazālī in Baghdad, and had studied under him. The author of legal works and of a juridical commentary on the Qurʾān (*Ahkām al-Qurʾan*) in which he refers to the teaching of his master, he contributed to the spread of his teachings in Spain. Subsequently Ghazālī had become interested in the method of *fiqh,* and had introduced into *fiqh* ways of reasoning that were drawn from Aristotle's logic, as is seen in his works *Al-Mustasfā* ("On the search for purity [in arguments]"), and especially *Al-Qistās al-mustaqīm* ("The Just Scale"), in which he shows that God Himself uses syllogisms in the Qurʾān. Such is the case, for example, with Abraham, who takes one of the heavenly bodies for his Lord when it rises, and then when it sets, says: "I do not like beings that disappear when they set" (6:76). If this verse is set in form, we have a syllogism concluding from the second figure in *Cesare:* My Lord does not set (= No Lord sets, no A is M). However, the sun sets (= every B is M). Therefore, the sun is not my Lord (= no B is A). Ghazālī undoubtedly belonged to another juridical school, Shafeism, which was opposed to Malikism from the beginning. This opposition, however, concerned primarily the use of traditions, and the problem of their coherence. It did not exclude— far from it, as a matter of fact—the common need for a method of dealing with Qurʾānic and prophetic texts. From this point of view, Averroes' Malikism, as we shall see, did not force him into strict and exclusive obedience, in the matter of legal doctrines, to the official teachings of a given school. And above all, it did not keep him from setting his own course in other areas. This is why Averroes was able to push his research on Aristotle's logic much farther, and in much more precise detail than Ghazālī had done. This is also why he was led, quite naturally, to study Aristotle's thinking as a whole, and to be interested in his philosophy of nature. Moreover, he had certainly been set on this path by masters who, like Abū Jaʿfar ibn Hārūn, knew both medicine and the thinking of the Ancients.

We thus see how Averroes could have been led to take an interest in Aristotle's logic, with problems on the methodology of law as his point of departure. It should nevertheless not be forgotten that he was oriented toward philosophy by a doctor, and consequently, that he also turned toward the sciences of nature. This approach through medicine is, moreover, characteristic of Muslim thinkers' introduction to Greek thought in general. Their master in this subject appears to have been Galen. Galen was undoubtedly first and foremost a medical doctor, and it was especially in this regard that history knows him. From his youth, however, he was a "regular" in the Platonic, Peripatetic, Stoic, and Epicurean schools—at a time of widespread philosophical syncretism. In his *De Libris Propiis,* he mentions Aristotle's *Categories* and his *Analytics,* and Plato's *Timaeus* and *Philebus.* Averroes knew Galen and quoted him, not without criticism, particularly in his *Great Commentary on Metaphysics.* He was thus introduced to the study of the philosophy of nature through Galen. But for all that, was he himself an observer of nature? He refers to natural phenomena in several commentaries, as in his book *On the Generation of Animals,* where he speaks of the influence the temperate climate of Cordoba has on hair, on sheep wool, and on temperaments. The influence of climate is noted, likewise, in the commentary on the *Meteorology:* "This is how it happens that the descendents of the Arabs and the Berbers who have taken up residence on Spanish soil change and take on the nature of an autonomous people." He was also led quite naturally to illustrate his ideas in his treatise on medicine, the *Colliget,* where he speaks about the purity of the waters of the Guadalquivir River. But these personal remarks that appear in the commentary cannot be considered as observations in the scientific sense of the word. However, in contrast to Plato, who turned primarily to mathematics and geometry, and who explained the world essentially in terms of numerical relationships and proportions, Aristotle was more a philosopher-observer of nature. This characteristic is found in Averroes, also, especially as a commentator on books like the *Physics,* the *Treatise on the Heavens, On Generation and Corruption,* and *The Generation of Animals.* The Cordoban philosopher was thus marked by this aspect of Aristotlean thought. Nor was an understanding of the value of experimentation foreign to him, although he was not personally an experimenter; we shall see that he engaged in some scientific research and that he regretted not having had more time to spend on it.

In 548/1153, Averroes was in Marrakesh, and we know from his commentary on *De Caelo* that he made astronomical observations there. Moreover, in his commentary on Book Λ of the *Metaphysics,* he notes the importance and the necessity of observation (*rasd*) of the movement of the heavenly bodies in the study of the sky, given the great number of geometrical and other explanations that the learned, both ancient and modern, offered in opposition to one another. He wrote: "In my youth I was hoping that it would be possible to bring this research to fruition; but at the advanced age where I presently am, I have lost hope." This text suggests that Averroes, at one point in his life, was truly oriented toward astronomical science. But no precise information is available in this regard, and we are forced to rely on conjecture. What is known is that Averroes was influenced by the philosophy of Ibn Bājja (Avempace), who had studied mathematics and astronomy: through him, he was able indirectly to be brought up to date on the return to a more Aristotelian vision of celestial phenomena among his learned contemporaries in Spain. But if we seek possible direct influence, we should turn rather to Ibn Tufayl, a philosopher-medical doctor who corresponded with Averroes and who had original ideas regarding the subject, according to the testimony of his disciple, the astronomist al-Biṭrūjī. What is certain is that the return to an Aristotelian vision of the heavens—in counterdistinction to the Ptolomeic system—among the astronomers of Spain must have yet further encouraged Averroes in his worship of Aristotle.

The same Ibn Tufayl, moreover, played a decisive role in Averroes's career. It was he who introduced Averroes to Abū Yaʿqūb Yūsuf, the second sovereign of the Almohad dysasty, the son of ʿAbd al-Muʾmin, who had been the disciple and successor of the Mahdī Ibn Tūmart. Certainly Abū Yaʿqūb had been educated in the theological doctrine of *tawḥīd,* divine unity, the basis of the Almohad movement. But during a stay in Seville, he was surrounded by philosophers, medical doctors, and famous poets; he gained cultural refinement, and became the friend and protector of the learned. The account of Averroes' interview with the caliph has been preserved for posterity. The prince asked him about the heavens: Had the heavens existed eternally, or did they have a beginning? Since the time of Plato's *Timaeus,* which teaches that the world had a beginning, but will have no end, this question had been bitterly debated. The assertion was that that which had a beginning must necessarily have an end. Aristotle had taken a position in favor of eternity. But his teaching ran counter to Qurʾānic doctrine regarding creation. The question was thus dangerous, and troubling to Averroes. Yūsuf understood the reason for this, and entered into discussion with Ibn Tufayl, showing tremendous knowledge of both the ancient thinkers and Muslim theologians. Thus encouraged, Averroes reentered the discussion and was able to show the breadth of his knowledge. This event appears to have taken place around 565/1169. We also know that the Commander of the Believers (the title that the Almohads had taken) had complained about the obscurity of the Arabic translations of Aristotle's texts. Ibn Tufayl asked Averroes to be in charge of the task of revision and clarification. We shall see the results when we examine the commentaries.

Averroes remained in favor throughout Abū Yaʿqūb's reign. During this period, he travelled extensively, visiting Seville, then Cordoba, always in his capacity as cadi. In 578/1182, he was in Marrakesh, where he replaced Ibn Tufayl as the first doctor for the caliph. Then he had bestowed upon him the title Grand Cadi of Cordoba. He remained in favor under the reign of Yaʿqūb al-Mansūr. It was only in the final years of the latter's caliphate that he fell out of grace. For what reason? It has been thought that the caliph, at the time engaged in battles against the Christians in Spain, thought it good to attempt to win the favor of the Malikī jurists, who continued to be powerful among the people under their jurisdiction. Averroes was banished to Lucena, near Cordoba, and his works were declared anathema; edicts ordered that they be burned, and the study of philosophy was forbidden. Under these sad circumstances, the philosopher was the victim of ignoble epigrams on the part of those envious of him. But when the caliph returned to Marrakesh, in a climate that was sensitive to the power of the *fuqahāʾ*, he revoked the edicts and called Averroes back. Unfortunately, the philosopher did not enjoy his return to favor for long, as he died in Marrakesh on 9 Safar 595/11 December 1198.

We cannot thus really accuse political power of having fought against philosophy in the name of religion. Averroes was not a martyr for freedom of thought; far from it, and if he needed to concern himself with the relationship between faith and reason, he did so in a fairly relaxed atmosphere, with no need of hiding his philosophical convictions for fear of upsetting the representatives of a threatening religious orthodoxy. For him, the problem of agreement between philosophy and religion was a problem that confronts everyone, one whose legitimacy a thinker should recognize and examine objectively.

CHAPTER I

Jurist

Averroes exercised the profession of cadi until nearly the last years of his life. What were the duties of a cadi, and especially of a Grand Cadi? A cadi (*qāḍī*) is an official invested with juridical authority. Since the caliph holds all legal powers, the cadi is named by him. In the Muslim West, particularly in Spain, the cadi is surrounded by a council of jurists whom he may consult. The principle of consultation (*shūrā*), based on the Qurʾān (cf. 42:38: "those whose affair is consultation among one another") is here applied each time a difficult case is presented. But the cadi is the judge, and he alone decides upon and pronounces the sentence. The cadi's competence includes both civil and penal litigation, and resides in the application of religious legislation (*sharīʿa*), in the form of specific legislative rules, the *furūʿ*, or "branches," drawn from the principles (*uṣūl*) of Qurʾānic law (*sharʿ*). It is here that the differences between schools play a role, since each Muslim is to be judged according to the school (*madhhab*) to which he belongs. In Spain, the "community judge" (*qāḍī ʾl-jamāʿa*) took on the title of Grand Cadi (*qāḍī ʾl-quḍāt*), in imitation of the Eastern Abbasid institution. He was responsible for the judicial administration, and for naming the cadis in the provinces. This is the nature of the functions, both civil and religious, that Averroes exercised.

ʿAbd al-Wahīd al-Marrakūshī, the 13th-century Maghrebin chronicler, relates an anecdote that shows Averroes fulfilling his duty as cadi. There was a renowned and erudite professor who was known as Wazaghi ("the gecko"). He had a follower whom people called Ghurnūq, a word meaning "crane," that was applied to a young man with a handsome face. Some of the professor's students suspected him of a secret and shameful attachment to the young man. This was not the case, since, as the narrator said, "God had saved him from such vice." But a student put this epigram into verse:

> O little lizard on the wall!
> A beautiful bird is your delight.
> Could such a thing be possible?
> You scramble walls, while he's in flight!

The professor took his complaint to Averroes, who inflicted corporal punishment upon the impudent poet. The narrator does not offer details of the punishment, but it could not have been anything other than what is called for by the Qur'ān, a punishment called *hadd,* which administers eighty blows with a whip to anyone guilty of *qadhf* for accusing a virtuous person of a shameful action without producing four witnesses. The Qur'ānic text (24:4) referred specifically to malicious gossip about virtuous women (*al-muhsanāt*): "To those who make accusations against chaste women without then producing four witnesses, administer eighty lashings and never allow them to make accusations again." Averroes undoubtedly extended this punishment to the men, thinking that the Qur'ānic verse applied to the letter of a specific case, but that it was also generalizable. The problem of the specific or general applicability of Qur'ānic verses is one with which the different works on *fiqh* deal, with some differences in solutions. We might note that in Mālikī law, application of punishment in this specific case did not take place unless a suit was brought against the perpetrator of the calumny. In fact, this is the way it happened in this case.

Averroes fulfilled his role as cadi conscientiously, and the religious nature of his duties—based on revealed Law—does not appear to have presented great problems for him. What interested him was the "rhetorical" aspect presented by the action in a judgment: the question of the value of someone's word, of his evidence, of his argument. Let us consider the *Commentary on Rhetoric* for clarification. At the beginning of the first book of this work, Aristotle speaks of the plaintiff, the judge, and the legislator with clear reference to Greek institutions. Averroes, as commentator, had to transpose Aristotle's ideas in order to make them meaningful in the legal order of Muslim procedures. Regarding the evidence that the speaker could offer in his personal speech, Aristotle wrote: "First of all there is the personality of the speaker." And here is Averroes' commentary: "The first evidence resides in the fact that he who speaks affirms his own qualifications, by virtue of which he deserves to be recognized as trustworthy." Averroes then relies on the Qurʾānic verse (7:68) in which God tells us that the prophet Hud told his people, "I am for you certain counsel." Here, thus, is one of Aristotle's ideas confirmed by the Qurʾān. This literal concordance suffices to guarantee the Muslim cadi the legitimacy of recourse to Greek philosophy.

Another indication of Averroes' attitude is his translation of the Greek word "legislator" (νομοθέτης) as *sāhib al-sharīʿa*, master of the Law. He establishes a correspondence between the Greek word *nomos* and the Arabic word *sharīʿa*, which refers only to religious Law. Ordinarily, the general idea of "law" in Arabic is expressed by the word *nāmūs*, from the Greek *nomos*. By translating *nomos* as he did, Averroes suggested that Aristotelian ideas relating to the practice of law could easily be transposed for the use of those who needed to apply God's law in Islam. It is true that he does not translate δικαστής, judge, by *qādī*, but by *hākim* (the general magistrate, with a root which means "wise"). It is possible that in Spain this name was given to the cadi to note his role as arbitrator. Actually, the word *hākim* is related to *hakam*, arbitrator, and the two words have the same plural (*hukkām*). But it is more likely that Averroes, a cadi himself, wished to draw a distinction between himself and the Greek judge.

It should be noted that Averroes, who did not know Greek, was dependent upon translators. It should not be assumed, however, that he was a passive recipient of the texts at his disposal. We shall see, with regard to his commentaries, that he did not hesitate to correct the translations he used, according to the meaning he felt they should have. He was not unaware of the possibility of imposing incorrect meanings or even misinterpretations. Some undoubtedly occurred, although when detected, they were corrected. We might also rightfully conclude that he was conscious of the value of the words he used and that he felt responsible for the way in which he used them.

Let us continue our examination of Aristotle's and Averroes' texts. Aristotle wrote: "It is clear that the plaintiff has nothing more to do than show that the litigious fact is, or is not: that it did or did not take place. But as for knowing whether it is important or trivial, just or unjust—things which the lawmaker has not defined—these are matters which the judge must know without learning them from the parties in question. It is therefore especially appropriate that well-formulated laws define everything that it is possible to define." Averroes paraphrased this text as follows: "He who wishes to establish something before the judges either establishes that the thing exists or does not exist, that is, whether it happened or not—which is the case when the lawmaker has defined that this thing, the object of the lawsuit, is important or trivial, just or unjust; or else he establishes both points: this is the case when the Law has not defined the matter under litigation [. . .]. But it must be traditional laws (*sunan*) which define whether a case is just or unjust, and which pass on to the judge the responsibility for deciding if the case is valid for a given person." We thus see what Averroes adds to Aristotle's text: the concept of recourse to traditional laws on matters that the Qurʾān does not address. It is in accord with these *sunan* that the cadi must arbitrate. Here we enter the heart of the problems posed by the bases of Muslim law: upon which traditions should the judge rely? We know that there are differences of opinion in this regard, particularly between the Mālikī and the Shafiʿī. The question is that of knowing upon which principle one either accepts a tradition as authentic, or rejects it as a forgery. This *hadith critique,* which constitutes, in Islam, the only form of historical criticism, was certainly of interest to Averroes. We shall see to what extent he dealt with it as a philosopher.

With regard to these questions, Averroes was actually a jurist, also, and he has left us a tome on law to which Robert Brunschvig has devoted a long article; its importance and originality make it worthy of mention here. The work's title is *Bidāyat al-mujtahid wa-nihāyat al-muqtasid,* meaning, "A beginning for him who makes a personal effort, and an end for him who refrains from such effort." The first of these expressions is of great importance: the *mujtahid* is he who makes a personal effort (*ijtihād*) in juridical research. This *ijtihād* is required for whoever is interested in the "principles of law" (the *usūl al-fiqh*). It is certain that one must begin here. Why? Because the Qurʾānic verses pose a number of problems of interpretation: for example, is a given text noting an obligation, offering simple advice, or giving permission? Should it be taken at face value as an absolute, general principle? Or, should it be looked at as a text with a particular meaning from which there will eventually be a need to generalize, with the general principle from which it derives teased out of it? The latter situation allows for an extension of the law from the specific case noted to other analogous cases not clarified to the letter, should a clear sign (*dalīl*) be discovered that allows either generalizing from a particular text, or particularizing from a text of general scope. This entails adhering to imam Shāfiʿī's method, or analogous reasoning, which is aimed at justifying logically the similarities that allow one to deduce from textually codified cases to those that are not, but which are comparable to them. There was a diversity of opinions on these questions, and Averroes examined all of them. The search for principles extended also to the study of traditions, and it was on this point that the doctors were in greatest opposition: should one, with the Mālikī, hold to the Medinese traditions either in totality or in part, or should others be allowed, provided their authenticity has been verfied? It was on this matter that differences in opinion (*ikhtilāfāt*) were the most frequent and the most numerous. The study of these differences in opinion formed its own branch of research in Islam, and it was to this branch of *ikhtilāf* that Averroes' work belongs.

The title of Averroes' work requires an explanation. Ordinarily, *taqlīd*, blind imitation, is opposed to personal effort, *ijtihād*. The *muqallid* is thus he who accepts the Law such as the Masters teach it. But Averroes set the *mujtahid,* who is concerned with *usūl al-fiqh*, in opposition to the *muqtasid*, who dispenses with this fundamental research and is content to study the applications derived from it, the *furūᶜ*. We have seen that Spanish Malikism was characterized by the importance given to treatises of *furūᶜ*. On this extremely serious point, Averroes was to stand out by working as a *mujtahid*, which is quite normal for a Muslim jurist worthy of the name, but also for a philosopher. Brunschvig wrote, in this regard, that Averroes wanted to place the accent on the "reasoning" aspect of this science. It is possible that he also wanted to show his connection with dogmatic theology, Ashᶜarite *kalām*. He had studied *kalām*, to which Ghazālī was connected, in his youth, but which he later criticized. The *Bidāya* seems to date from an earlier time—when Averroes was presented to the Almohad caliph in Marrakesh and named cadi of Seville—before he had written his great works on Aristotle's thought.

Brunschvig drew attention to an important fact. In the first edition of his work, Averroes did not deal with the pilgrimage to Mecca which is, however, one of the five "pillars of Islam." It was only later that he added a *Kitāb al-hajj* dealing with this obligation imposed insofar as possible upon every Muslim. The author offers an explanation that clarifies Averroes' attitude in the light of events of the day, as they related to the politics of the caliphate. The struggle against the Christians explains why emphasis was placed upon the *jihād* (holy war), which some consider a sixth pillar, and which was treated immediately after pilgrimage in legal works. Moreover, the distance, the difficulties, and the dangers of the trip from Spain to Mecca made the hazards of the pilgrimage comparable to the hazards of the holy war. Brunschvig writes in this regard: "At the time of Averroes, the Almohad caliph Abū Yaᶜqūb, reciting with his own lips a collection of Traditions to exalt both the holy war and to incite it, inserts among them a saying attributed to ʿAbd Allah ibn ʿUmar [a famous traditionalist, son of the caliph ʿUmar]: "A military expedition on the path to God [a *jihād*] is worth more than fifty pilgrimages." Later, Abū Yusūf al-Masnūr became interested in the East, intending to enter Egypt for the purpose of raising morals. It was thus polically important to restore the importance of the *hajj*. It was with this "foreign policy" situation in the background that Averroes reinserted a *Kitāb al-hajj* into his treatise. This interpretation is quite likely and has the advantage of showing that in the beginning, as well as at the apex of his philosophical activities, Averroes did not live in an ivory tower, content to profit from the caliph's favor, but that, in addition to his functions as cadi, he was attentive to the great political events in which Almohad Spain was involved.

What, then, does the *Bidāya* contain? It is a general treatise of Muslim law, not an exposé of Malikism, although it takes the school's point of view as its starting point. It examines all the problems of *fiqh* in a manner that Brunschvig calls "objective," that is, it reviews and critiques all the teachings, including Mālikī teachings themselves. It thus allows reasoning by analogy, all the while making clear that it is not a question of syllogism, but of inferring from particular cases to particular cases. But there is another form of reasoning, called *qiyās al-maʿnā*, which depends on "the meaning of the word," and which extends the scope of a word to whatever has no reason to be disassociated from it. Thus, when it is a question of dried dates in a text, all dried fruits are assimilated; or in the case of the woman referred to in a Qurʾānic verse, the case of a man. Let us remember that this is what Averroes had done in condemning the student to eighty lashings with a whip. He thus allowed the conclusion of one such *qiyās,* without seeing in it a real syllogism. Indeed, if it were put into syllogistic form, it could be seen that the case of men could not be concluded from the case of women:

> All women are human beings
> Such and such verse concerns all women
> thus, such and such verse concerns some human beings

It cannot be concluded, however, that it concerns all human beings—thus men—because not all human beings are women. The major (affirmative universal) premise of the syllogism is not convertible.

Averroes expands especially on the problem of traditions. There were great canonical collections, like those of Muslim and Bukhārī, which gathered the traditions held as "sound" (whence the name *saḥīḥ*, meaning "authentic," or "sound," that has been given to them). The essential criterion of authenticity of a tradition is, for Averroes, that it be found in one of these collections. We will not dwell on the much-debated question of the many forms that traditions can take. We will limit ourselves only to pointing out that a number of these problems had been examined by the Zāhirite, Ibn Hazm of Cordoba, whose legal doctrine was in favor among the Almohads, and which Averroes knew. One of these problems was that of knowing how to reconcile different traditions. Ibn Hazm made a well-thought-out exposé of it in his *Kitāb al-Muhallā*. The difficulties are resolved by extracting the particular from the general; or, by considering the chronology of the revelations, the later one abrogating the one that is earlier; or, when two opposing traditions are equally general, by looking for some sign that shows that they have different domains or conditions of application. It appears certain that, with regard to this particular point, Averroes remembered Ibn Hazm's solutions. Nevertheless, he takes great care to distance himself from Zāhirism, even to the point of allowing, at the level of the search for principles of law, for some intervention by reason, in the form of reasoning by analogy. On the other hand, Averroes condemns just as harshly as the Zāhirites those who rely on recourse to personal opinion, called *raʾy*, or simple "point of view," even if it is that of one of the Companions of the Prophet. As he says, the "statement of a Companion" (*qawl al-saḥābī*) takes no precedence over reasoning by analogy, even on the pretext that the Companion must be putting into words the teaching of God's Messenger. Similarly, the personal opinion of a doctor, regardless how illustrious he might be, could not constitute a law. From this point of view, the authoritarianism of certain Mālikī from Spain could be denounced and condemned. One should beware, however, of confusing this *raʾy* with the opinion (*zann*, δόξα) of the philosophers, which does have its place in the logical and methodological evaluation of knowledge. In this sense, as Averroes judges in the *Fasl al-maqāl,* the reasoning of the jurists has its value, although, compared with apodictic syllogism, it may only be probable, because it originates in opinion (*qiyās, zannī*).

We shall stop at one final question, one which is important in finishing up our background information on Averroes the jurist, along with Averroes the philosopher. It is known that when the traditionists report a hadith, they precede the text (*matn*) of the hadith with the list of all those who have reported it; this is the "chain of support" (*isnād*). The critique of authenticity is content to examine the value and the consistency of this chain. It might be expected that a philosopher's criticism of a hadith is based on the *matn* and its rational meaning (*maʿqūl*). Unfortunately, there is no unanimity in the understanding of the *maʿqūl* among the doctors who claim to discover it. In the face of the controversies that consequently arise, Averroes remains neutral. Brunschvig, nevertheless, notes a passage in which Averroes, with regard to the content of one of the traditions, thinks that nothing is opposed to "the Law's having [. . .] two meanings in mind; a utilitarian (*maslahī*) meaning and a cultural (*ʿibādī*) meaning." And he adds: "By 'utilitarian,' I mean that which relates to things of the senses, and by 'cultural,' that which relates to the purification of the soul (*zakāt al-nafs*)." This distinction appears to be one of the most important in the sense that it allows us to think that Averroes believed that a law could have a material and a spiritual significance, material to remind man that he is a being endowed with a body; spiritual, to remind him that he has a spirit. As for the unity of the law, it shows the unity of man in body and soul: he should not be content with the material observance of what the law prescribes, neither should he turn away from the world of the senses to be absorbed in a purely contemplative life. Thus, through law, the man of flesh is raised up toward the spirit, and the spiritual man is called back to his duties in the world. We would not be surprised if this concept were the deep conviction of Averroes, the jurist and the philosopher. We shall also see that he was interested in Revelation's relationship to the common man, to whom it brings a certainty and a consolation that he could never find through speculation. But this same Revelation reminds the philosopher that he should not forget man's legitimate needs, where "man" is understood in light of all his weaknesses outlined in the Qurʾān. Let it be borne in mind that this ideal balance that the Law establishes between the two components of human nature has always been claimed by Muslim exegetes as a characteristic specific to Islam. "We have made of you a community of a happy medium," as God says in the Qurʾān (2:123), meaning, from what the commentators say, in between two extremes: that of the Jews who put too much emphasis on the materialism of the law, and that of the Christians who take matter out, and see only the spiritual aspect.

Under these conditions, we understand that there was perfect harmony between Averroes, the jurist, and Averroes, the philosopher, and that his speculations on questions of law are supported by a logic whose objective is undoubtedly not to supply proofs by apodictic arguments, but to define a method of understanding texts, a method capable of presenting them as a whole and in an order satisfactory to reason.

CHAPTER II

Physician

We have seen the importance of medical studies in Averroes' education. It is not known whether he practiced medicine before being named private physician to the caliph Abū Yaʿqūb Yūsuf upon the recommendation of the philosopher and physician Ibn Tufayl. Nor is it known what kind of care he gave, or even if the caliph was at the time ill enough to have need of his physician's theoretical and practical knowledge. But the specialists in the medical arts among the Muslim Arabs thought (quite rightly, it might be mentioned) that their role consisted as much (or more) in preserving the health of their clients as in healing them of the diseases they contracted. One's diet, in the broad sense of the kinds of substances ingested, was of great importance. Particular attention was paid to food, and, after Dioscoridus, doctors studied what they called the "correction of foods," meaning that they attempted to neutralize the harmful effects of some foods by the salutary effects of others, or else to balance some foods by others. Medicines were likewise considered as correctives for foods and temperaments. Books dealing with these questions were abundant, and the treatises on medicinal herbs should be mentioned in particular. Averroes does not appear to have made observations that enriched this already rather widespread knowledge. But the numerous works that dealt with the topic were available for his consultation. Among others, he certainly must have known the opinion of his friend Avenzoar (Abū Marwān ibn Zuhr), of whom a work on foods and medicines is extant, *Kitāb al-aghdhiya*. Avenzoar first considers their effects depending on the season. For example, one should eat more in winter than in summer—because digestion is more active then—and nourish oneself with warm and dry foods. He goes on to examine the different kinds of breads, made from sorghum, beans, rice, chick peas, and so forth. Then he goes on to meats, dairy products, fruits, sugared dishes, honey, preserves, and finally drinks. He also offers a few principles of hygiene.

Averroes would have had at his disposal enough information to apply a treatment based on what was said regarding the effects of the different ingredients present in the *materia medica*. Was this enough to make him a true practitioner? He certainly knew how to take a man's pulse and examine his urine, but was he able to make a personal diagnosis? Would he have known, for example, like his friend Avenzoar, how to heal a man suffering from an intestinal problem, placing the blame on the water he drank that was drawn from an urn with a frog caught in it? What is sure is that he was not his friend's equal in this regard. He himself wrote in his treatise on medicine that, to have a good therapeutic foundation, it was essential to study Avenzoar's work. We should also note that it is incorrect to attribute to Averroes, as was done during the Renaissance, the idea that bleeding could be practiced on children without danger. Actually, he reported in the seventh book of his great treatise that it was Avenzoar who had bled his three-year-old son.

Might one think that Ibn Tufayl, who had recommended him to the caliph, had on this occasion given him some practical advice to assist him in the exercise of his new functions? Indeed, was Ibn Tufayl himself a true practitioner capable of providing this service? In this case, history provides no record. All that is known, via the historian from Grenada, Lisān al-Dīn ibn al-Khatīb (d. 776/1375), is that Ibn Tufayl supposedly taught medicine in Grenada and that he authored two medical works and a poem on medicinal herbs. He also had an exhange of views with Averroes regarding the chapter on medicines, to which the latter makes reference in his great treatise. But it is difficult to draw from these sparse data a conclusion that answers our question. What is most probable is that neither Ibn Tufayl nor Averroes, both of whom were physicians and philosophers, was superior to the other in the practice of medicine, regardless the quality of their theoretical knowledge.

It thus appears that Averroes' medical education was primarily book-based rather than practical in nature, but that it was nevertheless undertaken in some depth. We get an idea of this from the numerous commentaries that he authored on medical works: the commentary on the Urjūza, the poem on Avicenna's (Ibn Sīnā) medicine, the commentaries devoted to Galen's books on temperaments, causes and symptoms, fevers, medicinal herbs, and so forth. Whatever the case, if Averroes was not in his time in Spain a first-rate physician, there is no doubt that his medical studies and his interest in medicine served him when he wrote commentaries on the books of Aristotle that can be considered as treatises of natural history, such as the books on the *Parts of Animals*, and the *Generation of Animals* that he paraphrased. His knowledge of Galen was undoubtedly of great assistance to him.

A number of Averroes' medical works have been preserved, either in Arabic, or, especially, in Hebrew or Latin translations. We might cite, among others, the book *On Treacle*, a work on *The Differences in Temperament*, a volume on *Medicinal Herbs*, another on intermittent fever, and others still. All these topics had been the object of an abundant literature before Averroes, and even during his lifetime. Moreover, his great treatise, whose title in Arabic, *Kulliyyāt fīʾl-tibb* ("Generalities in Medicine"), was deformed by the Latin translators to *Colliget*, deserves a moment of our attention because it elucidates the extent of Averroes' works on medicine.

Let it be noted, first, that this title is the opposite of the title *Juzʾiyyāt fīʾl-tibb* ("Particularities in Medicine"). It is certain that Averroes must have thought about writing a work on medical practice following his book on theoretical medicine. In fact, he left this task to Avenzoar, and the information we have about Averroes, the physician, leads us to suspect that he felt his friend was more capable than he of carrying it out. It was actually at Averroes' request that Avenzoar composed his *Taysīr*, dealing with practical therapeutic applications. As Ibn Abī Usaybīʿa remembers in his work on the physicians, regarding this collaboration: "Averroes composed his book on generalities and asked Avenzoar to write his on particularities, so that, together, their two books would form a perfect work on the art of medicine (*sināʿt al-tibb*). This is why Averroes says at the end of his book: 'This is the teaching relative to the treatment (*muʿālaja*) of all kinds of illnesses, presented in the most concise form and with the greatest clarity that has been possible for us [referring here to the *kulliyyāt*]. After this part, we still had to deal with the healing (*shifāʾ*) of each of the illnesses with which each of the organs can be stricken. And, although this might not be necessary, since it is contained in the previously considered generalities, there is nonetheless in the study of particularities a certain complementary conclusion and a certain practical exercise (*irtiyād*), because through it the treatment of illnesses is approached as a function of each organ according to the methods of the authors of works on therapy (*al-kanānīsh*, pl. of *kunnāsh*). He who has mastered the generalities that we have written will be able to understand what is correct and what is erroneous in the therapeutic practice of the authors of *kunnāsh*.'" In fact, these works examined the parts of the body from head to foot, noting all the malfunctions and illnesses that could befall each of them, and pointing out the means of caring for them. One famous *kunnāsh* has come down to us, the *Paradise of Wisdom* (*Firdaws al-hikma*) by ʿAlī Rabbān al-Tabarī (3rd/9th century). It is certain that Avenzoar, a capable practitioner, was perfectly qualified to draw from generalities the appropriate treatment for each illness of each of the members of the body. What is characteristic of his *Taysīr* is his originality and his independence with regard to the traditions of his predecessors. He undoubtedly also dealt with questions relative to diseases specific to each organ, from the head to the foot. What is specific to Avenzoar, however, is his bringing in the results of his practical experimentation as support for his precepts and procedures. This characteristic, let there be no doubt about it, must have been pleasing to Averroes, and perhaps it even flattered what has been called his Hispanicism.

The *Colliget* corresponds to the first book of Avicenna's *Canon*. It is infused with the same spirit. Avicenna, after enumerating the different branches of theoretical medicine, actually adds that he who knows them has a right to be called a physician, even if he is not a practicing physician (*muzāwala*). From this point of view, which is certainly also that of Averroes, the author of the *Colliget* could, under Avicenna's authority, consider himself a physician. But, as in his writings on law, he integrated his medical knowledge into his overall philosophical perspective through his commentaries on Aristotle.

CHAPTER III

Commentator on Aristotle

It is difficult to differentiate between Averroes the commentator and Averroes the philosopher, except when it comes to the short, and perhaps even the medium-length commentaries, which are often paraphrases and generally do not express original ideas, even when they are laying the groundwork for the great commentaries. Nevertheless, we shall retain this distinction, realizing it may need to be slightly altered, for the simple reason that some of Averroes' works are not commentaries and that, even when they do use commentary, their goal is not to explain Aristotle's thought.

The fundamental remark to be made regarding the great *Commentaries* is that they are Averroes' works, even if their goal is understanding Aristotelian thought. Aristotle's Greek texts are often difficult to comprehend. And what are we to say about the translations that were no more than approximative, perhaps even erroneous, when they grappled with Greek idiomatic expressions, which was far from rare! It happened, moreover, that the commentator had a number of translations available; he compared one to another to determine the most satisfactory meaning that he could derive from them; then he made a choice and explained his preference. In cases where the Arabic text was obscure, or perhaps even incomprehensible, Averroes did not hesitate to rework it in light of what he did understand—and he often ended up with the precise meaning—or at least with a meaning that agreed with what was already known of the

Master's teachings through other channels. As a commentator, he never focused exclusively on isolated passages in his explications, but, rather, he always placed them into a wider context, so that his commentary was always organic and well argued. And finally, the combination of his reading of Aristotle, who often defines his thought by differentiating it from that of the other philosophers, and the personal knowledge he had of the works of the different Muslim *falāsifa* or *mutallimīn* (theologians) allowed him to identify quite accurately ideas specific to the Stagirite. This is why he was able to refer to a great number of Greek commentators who had been translated into Arabic, and to take issue with them regarding the meaning of specific passages. He referred likewise to the interpretations of other Muslim thinkers: Fārābī, Avicenna, Avempace. And, let us note, in particular, the careful attention he paid to philosophical vocabulary. He was of course able to make use of the definitions offered by the philosopher Kindi, and by Avicenna. Unlike his predecessors, he was not content, however, merely to define the philosophical meanings of the words used in their discipline; rather, he laid out an argument to justify his choice of a given word to transmit a particular concept. In what follows we shall find illustrations of all these characteristics of Averroes' commentaries.

It would be impossible to review here all of the great commentaries. To simplify things, while also guaranteeing that none of the important philosophical problems upon which Averroes touched in this huge part of his work is neglected, we shall limit ourselves almost exclusively to examining the *Commentary on Metaphysics* (which we shall cite according to the Bouyges editions, abbreviated B.), while simultaneously reviewing the fundamental concepts of Aristotelean thought.

Given the importance of names, we shall begin with an examination of the important ideas in the commentary on Book Δ of the *Metaphysics*. Averroes notes at the outset that the terms used by metaphysicians are "like the objects of knowledge with regard to the field of knowledge." These terms are those that are used to refer to one single thing under different circumstances;

they are not the more-ordinary terms, which may seem similar, but which are only considered in order to distinguish the meanings that are required, and which do not belong to any particular field of knowledge. "Thus, speculation on names is here the same as speculation on the varieties of objects (*aṣnāf al-mawdūʿ*) that the learned man considers." Averroes is clearly affirming the relationship between the name and the object from the outset.

Let us take the example of the word "nature" (*tabīʿa*), which Aristotle says comes from the verb φύεσθαι ("to be born, to grow"). The translator translated it using the Arabic *najama*, which means "to come into view, to come out, as in the case of a star" (the equivalent in Arabic is *najm*, pl. *nujūm*). Averroes replaced it with the verbs *namā* and *nashaʾa* (which both mean "to grow"). He noted that the Greek word is applied on the one hand to causes, and on the other to the causality of the causes for all growth. Which, then, is the meaning that best suits the metaphysician, and which is the first meaning? "Actually, the noun 'nature,' in its first meaning, is more general than the way the physicist uses it." The nature about which the metaphysician speaks is that whose causality he examines, whereas the physicist is interested in nature only as a cause caused by the causality of the metaphysical cause. However, it is by starting from physical causes that it is possible to elevate oneself to the causality of causes. This is why Avicenna was mistaken in thinking that the metaphysician first proves the existence of nature, and that the physicist is content to accept this proof and admit purely and simply the existence of nature as a principle of causation, thereby accepting the term "nature" in the sense that one says "that embryos, fruits, and grains grow." It is a constant idea in Averroes, in contrast to Avicenna, that without the concrete experience of the physicist, one would not be able to deduce from metaphysics the nature of the objects of physics. For him, metaphysics is not a science whose objective, by virtue of its fundamental dignity, lies beyond physics, but it is a science which comes after physics, and which is studied after physics. Thus the term meta-physics is translated in Arabic by separating the two components of the word: that which is after physics (*mā baʿd al-ṭabīʿa*).

Let us take the idea of cause: Averroes does not deal at length with material cause, a concept that is clearly illustrated. With regard to the second meaning of the word, formal cause, he is obliged to deal with an enigmatic translation in Arabic. Here is an English version of the passage (1013a25): "In another sense, cause is the form and the exemplary model (τὸ εἶδος καὶ τὸ παράδειγμα, *al-sūra wal-mithāl*), that is, the definition of quiddity (ὁ λόγος τοῦ τί ἦν εἶναι) and its genuses, like the relationship of two to one in an octave (τοῦ διὰ πασῶν)." The Arabic translation used by Averroes did not catch the particular meaning of the word *logos*, which is rendered as "word," and reflected neither the philosophical meaning of τὸ τί ἦν εἶναι nor the Greek expression διὰ πασῶν, which means ἡ διὰ πασῶν χορδῶν συμφωνία, or, "the harmony that passes through all the notes on the scale, thus the octave." Therefore, the translation, "that is, the word that indicates the act of existence (*kalima tadullu ʿalā kainūna*), like the relationship of two to one, brought back to that which is throughout the whole," does not make sense. Yet Averroes did understand the general meaning; here is his explanation: "Aristotle means that the form which is that of the genus is similar to the relationship of two to one; this relationship, in fact, is like the genus relative to melodic harmony (*naghma*) produced by the whole (*bil-kull*); it is actually the relationship of two to one that is the genus of this melodic harmony according to what is explained in the science of music." Let us note that Averroes did not catch the error in the translation of λόγος τοῦ τί ἦν εἶναι by "the word which indicates the act of existence," but that he interpreted it correctly when he said: "It is the cause that indicates the form appropriate for a thing and the form of its genus." This is how Averroes explains the image of formal cause.

Averroes does not spend much time on efficient cause, which does not present much difficulty. On final cause he writes: "It is the cause which is the accomplishment of the goal aimed at by the act of the agent [. . .]; it is what answers the question 'why?'

(*limā*, in view of what?). Where there is no final cause, the question of good is not asked." This supposes that there are effects which are not ends. Also, although one cause can be the cause of another, and the end, when it exists, determines the efficient cause, one cannot say with Avicenna that the final cause is the cause of the causality of the efficient cause, since there can be efficient causes that act in the absence of a final cause. Movement can thus be a means for attaining an end, but there is not an end in itself: "As for the causes which are the seed, the doctor, the step, and everything that is the agent of an action, they all lead back to the cause which is the beginning of a change following a fixity and a state of rest; and this cause is called movement." The effect of a movement is no more than a change, not its final result. It must be noted that Aristotle's text spoke of a "cause which is a beginning of a change or of rest," that is, that the efficient cause can produce a movement or the stopping of a movement. For Averroes, the efficient cause changes rest into movement. This difference in point of view is important, and is to have consequences in astronomy and in physics.

To end this brief look at the personal role that Averroes plays in his commentary, let us now turn to the idea of being (τὸ ὄν). The word used by the translator is *huwiyya*, and Averroes makes an interesting remark on this point: "You must know that the noun *huwiyya* was not a form of an Arabic word at the beginning of the language; some translators simply felt forced to use it, and derived it from the particle of liaison which for the Arabs marks the attachment of the predicate to the subject in its substance as subject (*al-mawdūʿ fī-jawharihi*): it is the particle *huwa* (he, him) in the expression: Zaid, he [is] an animal, or a man [. . .]. Having found the particle used in this way, they derived a noun from it following the custom the Arabs have of deriving a noun from a noun; even although they do not derive nouns from particles." The translators thus treated the particle, *huwa*, like the equivalent of the copulative *esti* ("is") which does not exist in Arabic, where the nominal sentence with two terms, the inchoative and the enunciative (*mubtada* and *khabar*: Zayd—man), is normal usage. This neologism corresponds to the Arabic *mawjūd*, which means "[the] being," but which is in reality the passive past participle of the verb *wajada* (to find). The *mawjūd* is thus etymologically "that which is found." Philosophically, this term runs into serious objection: "The noun *mawjūd* certainly does belong to the Arabic language, but it is a noun derived [from a verb], and since nouns [thus] derived only refer to accidents, one must then imagine that it serves, in the sciences, to refer to the essence of a thing, that it denotes only an accident [of this essence]. This is what happened to Avicenna." Actually, for Avicenna, being, in the sense of existence, is an accident which occurs to each of the categories, including substance. The categories, quantity, quality, and so forth, do certainly exist in substance, but, for this to be true, substance must exist. It does not, however, exist by itself; its essence does not envelop existence (which takes place only in the case of the Being necessary in Himself); it must receive existence, and existence is thus that which happens to it, meaning that it is an accident. At the level of a simple grammatical reflection regarding a word, Averroes takes a position on the idea of being, which is in opposition to Avicenna. We shall see the numerous consequences that follow, philosophically, from this initial reflection.

We shall examine three groups of important questions: (1) those which relate to being; (2) those which relate to the world; (3) those which relate to, or are associated with, knowledge.

Problems Related to Being

Despite the flaw that *mawjūd* presents, Averroes preferred this word, and it is the word that he would use. If this word, he said, "denoted in the language of the Arabs what the word 'thing' (*shayʾ*) denotes, it would be more appropriate than the word *huwiyya* to refer to the ten categories." Using it, it would suffice to understand nothing of the fact that it is derived. But we must here emphasize the relationship that should exist between the being thus expressed and the thing. Avicenna also remarked that being is indefinable; otherwise, it would be necessary to say that being is something (*mā*), or a thing (*shayʾ*), that is. However, Avicenna wanted to say that all objects of thought are something, that is to say, beings. In contrast, it appears that by "thing" Averroes meant a concrete object of experience. Being is not first of all a thing that someone thinks, but a thing that is given. In this concept of being, he is certainly closer to Aristotle than Avicenna is. Also, at the same time he gives a meaning to the passive past participle *mawjūd:* being is that which is given, that which is found, and that which is not thought until after it has been found.

The origin of the word *huwiyya* is of interest, since if in Arabic it is taken from that which serves as a copulative in a judgment of attribution, and if it denotes the ten categories, we immediately understand that it denotes them according to an analogy of attribution: the noun of being is not univocal, and is not applied to all beings with the same single meaning; but it is not a pure homonym as if, for example, there were no difference between the being of an animal and the being of a number or of a color, any more than there is between the eye and a spring, which in Arabic are both denoted by the same word, ʿ*ayn*. But among all the ways the word "being" can be used there is an analogy of attribution founded on the fact that everything that is called "being" is such only by attribution to a subject which is the same in all cases: substance. "The noun of being is one of those that are said to be relative to a single thing; those are the nouns that are known in the science of logic by the fact they are said to be according to anteriority or posteriority, because they are intermediary between univocal nouns and nouns with a variety of meanings." (B. 302, 13–16; 303, 3). Thus, one cannot say that being is a genus, or else it would be definable in a univocal manner. On this point, Averroes agrees with Avicenna. But for Avicenna, being, existence, since it is an accident that is received, is necessarily received to the same extent as what receives it, according to the adage: *Quidquid recipitur, ad modum recipientis recipitur.* This idea led to what has been called the analogy of proportionality: the being of substance is to the substance what the being of quality is to quality, what the being of quantity is to quantity, and so forth. On the contrary, for Averroes, being is said to be by anteriority to substance, and by posteriority to the other categories that are all predicated on substance (cf. B. 308, 17). Nothing that is, other than substance, is a being in the absolute sense of the word (B. 1414, 8 ff.).

However, being, as being—that is, insofar as it is not the being of some thing—can be divided. But since it is not a genus, and thus, since it has no specific differences, how is this possible? Similarly, as being—that is, taken absolutely—it would not be capable of being divided relative to the categories. Avicenna had admitted an analogy on this point. In his third part of the *Kitāb al-Najāt,* he wrote, "The division of being into categories is like division by specific differences, even although such is not the case; its division into potentiality and actuality, into one and multiple, into eternal and temporal, into perfect and imperfect, into cause and effect, and all other divisions of this sort, is like division by accidents, such that the categories are like species, and the other divisions like accidental differences. . . ." In reality, these resemblances explain nothing, except that they allow Avicenna to construct a metaphysics of Being in actuality, one, eternal, perfect, first cause of all that exists. As we have seen, it is not in this sense that Averroes conceives of metaphysics.

Averroes wrote: "The fact of being substance or accident is the first division that divides up being as 'being'" (B. 759, 16). He notes clearly that this division comes from metaphysics and not from physics. Actually, the science of nature studies substance as a body and ends up at knowledge of prime matter, of natural forms, and of the first movement, while this metaphysical division, in distinguishing substance from accident, "ends up at knowledge of the first form of all beings and of the final end." It shows, so to speak, the *raison d'être* of beings.

Being is further divided into that which is in potentiality and that which is in actuality. On this subject, Averroes makes a remark that might pertain to all the divisions of being: "That which belongs in common to all genuses of being (to all categories) falls under the domain of the concomitants (*lawāhiq*) of being as 'being.'" However, the divisions in question are present in each of the categories. We thus see that it is not by starting from speculation on being as being that Averroes conceived of the divisions of being. Rather, his starting point was observation of the existence of these divisions in each of the categories, that is, in each of the beings that depend upon them and are accessible to experience. Thereafter, he extended these divisions to being as being. We thus find, again, the importance accorded to empirical data as a point of departure for speculation on being.

On the matter of the one, it is an error to believe, as some of the Ancients did, that it has only one meaning and that it denotes the concrete substance (*al-jawhar al mushār ilayhi* = the substance that can be pointed to with one's finger) assimilated to being. The divisions of the one are equal in number to the divisions of being. Averroes follows Aristotle closely on this, and we shall not belabor the point. But two other ideas related to being are that of the necessary (*wājib*) and that of the possible (*mumkin*). Averroes wrote: "All potentiality and all that is possible are potentialities for the existence and for the non-existence of a thing; they are not a potentiality for only one of these two opposites." Actually what has potentiality for one of the two opposites does not have potentiality for the other, since that for which there is no potentiality would not be able to exist, and that which would not be able to exist is impossible (*mumtaniʿ*). And when one of the two opposites is impossible, the other is necessary, and consequently it is not possible, since the necessary is the opposite (*didd*) of the possible. This important idea had already been seen in Avicenna. Confusion arises when people take the possible for the opposite of the impossible. Avicenna introduced another idea, that of the *darūrī*, which is applied to that whose existence is imposed inevitably; thus the necessary and the impossible are opposed as the two poles of the *darūrī*: the necessary is that whose existence imposes itself, and the impossible is that whose non-existence is imposed inevitably. The possible is that which can equally exist and not exist (B. 1141, 1). There is a relationship between the idea of potentiality and that of the possible. The idea of potentiality is not used absolutely (*bi itlāq*), but relative to actuality, and one cannot define it except in relation (*bi-idāfa*) to its actuality. Likewise, the possible is not understood except in relation to actuality (B. 1158–1159). This is why it is not only an object of logic, but an object relative to being, and thus an object of metaphysics.

It must therefore be noted that Averroes places the possible in relation to being in potentiality, and that he has an ontological, and not simply logical, conception of it. Interpreting a difficult passage of the *Metaphysics* (Θ, 1047b3), he writes: "If that which one calls possible (*mumkin*) and consequent (*lāzim*) in what concerns potentiality (*quwwa*) and possibility (*imkān*) is anterior [in time] to actuality, then it is clear that it is not possible for something possible ever to come into actuality. When one posits that a possible thing will not be, which is Plato's teaching, it follows that one no longer has the means of positing the impossible." There is thus a reality of the possible: a possible that cannot become real, cannot be distinguished from the impossible.

In clarifying Aristotle's thought, Averroes thus touches on a serious problem that has divided such philosophers as Leibniz and Spinoza: is the best of all possible worlds really the only one that exists, other possible worlds existing only in the thought of a purely logical existence? Or, is only one world possible, the one that actually exists, with everything possible being real? In other words, are there essences that are possible only, and that exist only if they receive existence through the effect of a cause exterior to them, without having in themselves the real potentiality to exist? On this point Averroes is opposed to Avicenna's teaching that there are in this world beings that are possible through themselves and necessary through something other than themselves, except in the movement of the sky. "But that there exists a thing possible in its essence, whose existence may be necessary through something other than it, this is not possible, since it is not possible for the same thing to be of a possible existence through its essence and to receive necessary existence from another" (B. 1632, 1f.).

Aristotle said that we should not identify what is false with what is impossible (Θ, 1047b12). Averroes notes in this regard that those who say that the possible as such is that which cannot enter into existence are those who deny that potentiality precedes actuality. In contrast to them, Averroes maintains that the possible is connected to being in potentiality. Consequently, a distinction must be made between that which is false because it is impossible, and that which is false even though it is possible. It is false to posit in actuality that which exists only in potentiality, but it is not, for all that, impossible, because that which is false and impossible is that in which there is no potentiality. As Aristotle said, "it is false that you are standing up right now, but it is not impossible," precisely because you are standing in potentiality. If, on the other hand, as Averroes continues, we suppose that A is corrupted in actuality and that A is not corrupted in potentiality, that is, that there is not in A the possibility of corruption, that implies according to [the Darapti method of] the third figure of the syllogism, that something in which there was no possibility of corruption has been corrupted; in effect, we would have:

Major: A is corrupted [in actuality] (a);
Minor: A is [in potentiality] not corruptible (a);
Conclusion: Thus, something non-corruptible [in potentiality] is corrupted [in actuality] (i), which is to say that something has been corrupted in which there was no possibility of corruption.

As it has been posited that this conclusion, being false and impossible, could not follow from a possible premise, we see that the premise from which this impossibility follows is that which states that that in which there is potentiality for corruption will absolutely not be corrupted because of this. This is explained by the principle that the impossible does not follow from the possible. This, Averroes adds, is how the thesis is refuted that a thing that has a beginning in being remains eternally. He almost certainly has in mind Plato's teaching that the Universe has a beginning, but is eternal. Every being that has a beginning is a possible being that is preceded by its being in potentiality. Actually, if the world exists, it is because it is possible, or in other words, it has a potentiality for being. But when it exists, it is a real possible, meaning that if it exists in actuality it has not, for all this, become necessary and would not be able to subsist without end. There is no pure act which alone can be eternal. We shall see that Averroes, following Aristotle, proves that the world is eternal *a parte ante* and *a parte post* at the same time. Such is, then, the connection between potentiality and the possible (B. 1144, 3f.).

Let us note that some theologians, especially those of what is known as the Muʿtazilite School, raised the question of knowing whether God creates all that He can create. Most thought that such was not the case, because then creation would exhaust His potentiality. The possible thus exceeds the real. It is the object of the active, infinite potentiality of God, his *qudra*. This object, which is that upon which His active potentiality acts, is called *maqdūr ʿalayhi*. It is not because a possible has in it a potentiality in the Aristotelian sense of the word (*quwwa*, not *qudra*) that it is the object of the active potentiality of God. Everything depends on God and on God alone; beings are pure nothingness before they are created by the divine power that is perfectly transcendent to them. Now, for Averroes, there is no pure nothingness; nothingness is always relative to existence (B. 391, 7; 801, 12; 1601, 16). Consequently: "A being (the being: *al-kawn*) proceeds from that which becomes being, that is, from that which is on the way to being. For the existent in actuality, from which a being is fashioned, is in reality opposed to nothingness, and it is not possible for a being to proceed from nothingness; that is, it is not possible for nothingness to be that which becomes being (*al-mutakawwin*)" (B. 27). There are no possibles in nothingness. But Averroes' God, remaining quite close to Aristotle's, is not a creator in the Qurʾānic sense of the word, so the question of creative power and the will to create does not come up for him.

Problems of the World

The doctrine of being that is founded on the analogy of attribution had the immediate consequence of moving substance into the foreground of research, since it is the first analogue of being. Averroes follows Aristotle quite closely on this point. All that is, is substance, or exists in a substance. "Substance is in reality the existent being" (B. 1406, 7). Given this, "it is necessary to know that there are two kinds of substances: the substance that subsists through itself and which cannot be deprived of the accidents that it carries, and the substance that subsists through itself, devoid of all accidents. The first is sensible substance, the second is intelligible substance" (B. 1533, 15–1534, 2).

Averroes is careful to make the distinction between the study of substance in physics and in metaphysics. Physics extends its research "to the principles of the body as [something] natural, that is, in the sense that it is a being existing at rest or in motion, while metaphysics considers it only in that it is a substance subsisting through itself, since the first division of being, as being, is that a thing is substance or accident. Metaphysical research leads to the first form, which is that of all existing beings, and to their final end, while research in physics leads only to knowledge of prime matter, to natural forms, and to the prime mover" (B. 759, 12–760, 3). It is concrete apprehension of individual bodies from the outset that first gives the idea of substance which is thus the sensible substance; but it does not really say what the quiddity (*māhiyya*) of the substance is, what makes the sensible substance, form or matter, in motion or in rest, be a substance. So Aristotle wonders, Averroes tells us, if there are separate (*mufāriqa*) substances other than sensible substances that would be the cause (*ʿilla*) of sensible substances, as the partisans of mathematical forms (*al-suwar al-taʿlīmiyya*) would have it. In reality, however, for Averroes as well as for Aristotle, numbers come out of quantity, and refer to a numbered substance in relation to which they are accidents. Substances are undoubtedly not complete except in the sense that they are finished "in respect to size and quality" (B. 625, 10). They can thus be described through the accidents they carry. But they are something different than the sum of their accidents. Moreover, mathematical forms are called forms only to the extent that they give form to a matter or a combination of matter and form, that is, a sensible substance. The cause of a substance could not be found in its accidents, but in another substance.

What makes a substance a substance must therefore be sought elsewhere. This question is asked not only for sensible substances, but also for separate substances. And what, in fact, are separate substances? They are the cause of celestial bodies (*al-ajrām al-samawiyya*), and their existence can only be explained by motion (B. 771, 15; 1423, 11). Their number is equal to that of the movements of the stars, since they are movers "by virtue of the fact that the passivity due to matter does not touch them, since their being is immaterial and is in a superior state" (B. 1080, 9–1081, 3). As driving forces, these separate substances can rightly be called gods, according to an ancient tradition. Averroes uses the word "gods" (*āliha*), in the manner of Aristotle, who speaks of the *theoi*. Avicenna prefers to speak of angels, and a number of Christian philosophers do likewise. But it might be that, for them, there was a desire to bring philosophical teachings into accord with Revelation. Such was not the case for Averroes. This kind of concordism was of no interest to him, and the fact that he retained the word "gods" in the plural, as in Aristotle, is evidence of this.

Separate substances are distinguished from sensible substances because they are the substances of the celestial spheres, the causes of the movements of the stars, and because this circular and eternal movement is of a different kind than natural rectilinear upward and downward movements. On all these points, Averroes' commentaries add nothing important to Aristotle's texts. The sublunar world is the world of generation and corruption, which makes it different from the celestial movements. This supposes that the matter of the spheres is different from that of this world. Averroes dealt with this question in his *De substantia orbis*. In his Commentary, he wrote: "The sky has a nature that exists and is specific to it, in that it is neither created nor corruptible, since the sky exists continually in the three divisions of time, the present, the past, and the future" (B. 108, 12). "It has a local constituent element (ʿ*unsur makānī*) and is not generable or corruptible" (B. 1686, 15). The celestial bodies are the spheres that carry the stars, and in this sense it can be said that there are as many skies as there are spheres. But there is an eternal "first sky" through which the movements of the other celestial bodies are accomplished. This 'first sky' is moved by the desire that it has for the prime mover, that is, the desire to resemble it to the extent of its capabilities" (B. 1606, 13). Here, Averroes does nothing more than follow what Aristotle says, while developing the idea: "The thing that is chosen for itself and desired among these separate driving principles, each of which has a single, simple meaning as a basis for the body that it moves, is the thing that, among all principles, is at the height of excellence, simplicity, and unity. And the goal of this statement is to distinguish the first principle from the other separate principles which, of their own accord, appear to be chosen and desired for something other than themselves; what I mean by this is the principles of the other celestial movements, with the exception of daily movement. Regarding the mover of this latter movement, it appears to be chosen and desired for itself, since the whole universe is moved toward it [. . .]. It is thus the mover which is chosen and desired for itself by the whole universe" (B. 1604, 4 ff.). Consequently, "this prime mover, being immobile, moves the first moving body [the sky of fixed bodies] like the beloved moves his lover without being moved himself." Here Averroes takes up one of Aristotle's images again; but there is another one, that of the relationship between a king and his subjects, from which he would take inspiration for his *Tahāfut*, to mark an analogy between God, Who commands, and creation, which obeys.

Such is the architecture and the functioning of the universe for Averroes, in perfect harmony with Aristotle's teaching. Even with regard to the movements of the planets, it was easy for him to remain in accord with the Aristotelian vision, for, as we have seen, it was at the time regaining favor among the astronomers of Spain. Moreover, Averroes was aware of the history of Greek astronomy, and in his commentary he wrote about the teachings of Eudoxus of Cnidus and Callippus, adding his personal thoughts regarding the Stagirite's views on them. But what is more important is the opposition to Ptolemy, which is easily understood as soon as one accepts the thesis that the planets are fixed on spheres which are not mathematical fictions, but rather substantial realities. The real existence of eccentric spheres that cut into one another became both impossible and inconceivable. Avicenna himself ran into this difficulty. Under these circumstances, the apparent movements of the planets can be nothing more than the result of the combined movements of homocentric spheres, and, since there is no void in the world, in order to account for the aberrant movements of planets, it became necessary to introduce "compensatory" spheres which, turning the wrong way (ἀνελίττουσαι σφαίραι), assure both an indirect contact with the sphere of the superior planet and dependence in its movement on the sphere that carries the inferior planet. We get an idea of the complexity of what might be called the representation of this result.

Aristotle's text in the *Metaphysics* on this point happens to be far from clear; the Tricot translation (II, p. 181) does nothing to clarify it, and the Arabic translator's rendering of it is quite inexact. Thus, "the spheres which turn backwards" became "the spheres that turn with a motion turning in a spiral" (*ukar allatī tadūru bi-dawr lawlabī*). The translator did not understand the meaning of the verb ἀνελίττω, which he brought back to its root, ἕλιξ, the meaning of which is indeed "spiral," or "helix" (*lawlab*), but which for astronomers simply means "circular movement of the stars." Under these conditions, there was little to expect from the commentary, except that Averroes attempted to correct the text, and to give it an acceptable meaning. He wrote, "All these added [compensatory] spheres make each of the first spheres [those which carry a planet] turn in a direction different from that in which it turns [by itself]. The result of this is that the heavenly body [the planet] is seen to return to its first position relative to the circle of the zodiac. Then we see it begin to straighten out. Aristotle means that it is as if the heavenly body were forced to take on, as a result of the opposing movements of these spheres, a spiral motion."

These examples will suffice to show the commentary work that Averroes did on the problem of the world.

The Problem of Knowledge

Knowledge can be looked at from its starting point, or from its endpoint. At its endpoint, it is the apprehension of objects of intellect. At the starting point, all begins for Averroes, as for Aristotle, with what is clearest for man, that is, with sensation and sense perception. But it is especially the problem of intellectual knowledge that draws our attention, since it is through his ideas on this subject that Averroes had the greatest audience, and was the object of the strongest criticism regarding the so-called doctrine of the unity of the intellect. Renan wrote in *Averroès et l'averroïsme:* "All Averroes can be summed up in two intimately connected teachings [. . .]: the *Eternity of matter,* and the *Theory of the intellect.*" We will spend time only with the second of these, and with its consequences.

Averroes' ideas are formulated especially in his commentaries on the *Treatise on the Soul,* even though the influence of Fārābī, and, even more so, Avempace, are not negligible here. In the third book of *De Anima* (430a10 ff.), Aristotle makes a distinction between two intellects, one of which is passive and in potentiality, and the other active and in actuality. The first can become all the objects of intellect by thinking them, the other allows them to be apprehended as objects of intellect, and is analogous to light that allows one to see in actuality the colors that are visible in potentiality. However, this analogy raises a problem, since light is on the one hand separated from colors, and on the other it is in the colors that it makes visible. Like light, the active intellect is thus in one sense separated, and in one sense it is not, which is why Aristotle wrote: "Once it is separated (χωρισθείς) it is no longer anything but what it is essentially, and this alone is immortal and eternal." Consequently, the passive intellect and the light in it from the active intellect would be perishable. But there is a difficulty that did not escape Averroes in this text, and one that vexed the commentators. Can one conclude that the active intellect, being separated from individuals, and as such immortal and eternal, is a single and impersonal entity for all men?" Does Aristotle's teaching lead to such a simple consequence, and is this the way that Averroes understood it? Renan wrote: "Certainly, if there is a revolting absurdity in the world, it is the *unity of souls,* as people have pretended to understand it, and if Averroes had ever been able to uphold such a teaching literally, Averroism would deserve a place in the annals of dementia, and not in those of philosophy." It is certain that Averroes' thought, as early as in his commentaries, and especially in his personal reflection, was much more elaborate. It is this that we shall examine by carefully following the numerous analyses of his paraphrase of *De Anima* (*Talkhīs kitāb al-nafs*).

Regarding the soul in general

In his paraphrase of the *Treatise on the Soul,* Averroes takes as his point of departure the definition of the soul as the form of a natural body endowed with organs. Every corporal being (*jism*) is composed of matter and form; however, in an animal, matter is the organic body (*badan*), and form is the soul. Given this circumstance, "the natural forms are the first entelechies (*al-istikmālāt al-uwal*) of the bodies of which they are the forms; whence the definition of the soul as the first entelechy of a natural body endowed with organs." The second entelechies, the results of activity and passivity, are consequences of the first entelechy, since they are drawn from it. However, Averroes remarks, this definition applies indistinctly and ambiguously to all the faculties of the soul. "Thus entelechy in nutritive potentiality has a different meaning than in sensible potentiality, in imagination, and, even more so, in what is said about it, by homonymy, regarding the rational soul." It follows that the unity of the soul that seems apparent in the definition is not a real unity. Already in this commentary we see the appearance of the idea that the general definition of the soul as the form of a living body needs to be seriously amended when it comes to the human soul.

The nutritive soul

Beings in potentiality do not pass into actuality except under the action of a mover in actuality. Let us consider the case of the nutritive soul: bread is a food in potentiality, and the mover is the nutritive soul which, by acting on the appropriate organs, turns it into food in actuality. But we are here dealing with a close potentiality; on the other hand, the elements are foods only in distant potentiality, and the nutritive soul is thus not their mover. It has action only on a substance that is in one sense different from food, and in another sense similar, meaning that it acts only on a substance that is appropriate at the end of its action. But for this it makes use of an organ of the body that it alone has the capability of getting to act. We shall limit ourselves to pointing out that nutrition is like matter for two other faculties, that of growth and that of reproduction.

The sensitive soul and its relationship to the nutritive soul

The sensitive faculty is passive, since it is sometimes in potentiality and sometimes in actuality. What, then, is its mode of existence, what is its mover, and how does it receive movement? In his book on animals, Aristotle dealt with conditions far removed from the existence of this faculty. As for the immediate mover, it is clear that it is the sense objects in actuality that act on the organs of the appropriate senses. How then does this faculty receive the setting into motion that comes from these sense objects? In an animal's nutritive soul there is a disposition (*istiʿdād*) that is not present in plants. But there is a difference between the potentiality that bread has to become a food and the potentiality that sense objects have to become sensation in actuality. The nutritive faculty, acting upon appropriate organs, transforms bread into a food. But the sensible faculty does not transform a sense object into sensation, since, as a disposition in the nutritive soul, it is itself transformed into sensation by the sense objects that give the disposition its final perfection. This is why, for example, the existence of color inside this faculty is not its existence on the outside. Actually, "its existence in its matter outside the soul is that of an essence divisible according to the divisions of matter; as for its existence in the sensible faculty, it is possible that it is perfectly realized in a very large body, just as it is in a very small body, according to a single mode of existence and in a unique subject [the soul], just as the lens of the eye, despite its small size, can take in half of the celestial sphere." Consequently, this sensible faculty can receive two opposites at the same time perfectly well, just as vision takes in both black and white at the same time. "This is why, through this faculty, it happens that [external] sense objects exist with a nobler existence than they have in their matter outside the soul." In short, the external sense objects, by acting on the organs of the body and putting them into motion, are the driving forces that make the inherent disposition of the nutritive animal soul pass into perfect actuality (*istikmāl*) and transform it into the sensible faculty that apprehends them in the form of sensation. Let us thus note that, thanks to this disposition, there is perfect continuity in an animal between the nutritive faculty and the sensitive faculty, so that these faculties form a unity in the animal. Averroes concluded that this perfect actuality (*istikmāl*) has no meaning (*maʿnā*) other than that of the existence of sense objects separated from their matter. Nevertheless, in sensation, the sense object keeps a particular relationship with matter, and through this takes on the meaning of a particular.

Thus, sensation apprehends only the sensible form separated from matter. This form is separated sometimes in potentiality, and sometimes in actuality; consequently, it is necessarily something that happens in a contingent (*hādith*) fashion, since "potentiality is the most significant of the causes of contingence (*hudūth*)." In effect, "a potentiality cannot be eternal (*azaliyya*), or else the sense objects in potentiality would not need to be apprehended by a sense [which actualizes them], with the result that the act of sensing them would be identical, whether they were absent or present." The presence of objects of sensation to corporal organs is necessary in order for them to be apprehended by the sensitive soul. It is only then that the imagination will be able to form an image of them in their absence, on the basis of sensation, and suppressing all reference to their matter. This indispensable role accorded to the sensitive soul in knowledge runs counter to the Platonic teaching of exemplary ideas. It runs very much in the direction of pure Aristotelian thought.

Common sense

There are five senses that belong, each separately, to the sensitive soul. But since there are common sense objects, it appears as though they come out of a single faculty, which is itself common. Averroes puts order into Aristotle's too confused words on this question. These sense objects are common in that they can be apprehended either by all the senses, like movement and number, or by two of them at the same time, like size and shape, apprehended by sight and touch simultaneously, even though the visual apprehension of a figure is different from its tactile apprehension; but we can apprehend the otherness of sense objects in each of the senses, and we judge, for example, that an apple, perceived as a whole by sight, has a color, a smell, a taste, a shape. The faculty that *judges* that these sensibles are different from one another is necessarily a unique faculty.

Another argument in favor of the existence of a specific faculty is drawn from the fact that each of the five senses, besides its own specific sense object, apprehends the fact that it apprehends it. "The senses sense the act of sensing; it is as if the act of sensing itself were the object of this apprehension, since its relationship to this faculty is the relationship of the sense objects to each of the senses; this is why this act cannot be related to only one of the five senses, or else the sense objects in themselves would be the acts of sensing themselves. Thus, for example, the object of the faculty of sight is color, and that of the other faculty is the apprehension itself of the sight of color, and if this act of sensing belonged to the faculty of sight, color would be identical to the very act that apprehends it, which is absurd." From all these observations, it follows that there exists a single faculty which is common to all the senses. It is single on the one hand, and on the other it is multiple, which we can understand through the image of a circle: radii are multiple from the point of view of their extremities that touch the circumference, but they are single at the point where their extremities join in the center of the circle. Likewise, the movements that leave the sense objects are numerous relative to the sense objects themselves and to organs; but they are one in the fact that they end at a single faculty which senses that it senses all the sense objects.

The aim here is to show that there exists a unique faculty that is reflective; it apprehends the act of sensing (*ihsās*) in each sensation, and can thus apprehend in it common sense objects as well as their differences. Thus when one senses that one senses the taste of an apple and one senses that one senses its color, one senses that the color is not the taste, even though the two sensations are registered at the same time. On the contrary, when one senses that one senses a shape and one senses a quantity or a movement, one senses that this quantity or this movement is the quantity or the movement of the shape, and this is the way that common sense objects are sensed. This is why there is already at this level a kind of implicit judgment that Averroes notes well when he says, regarding this faculty, that it judges (*al-quwwa allatī taqdī*). Consequently, thanks to common sense, tightly connected in the sensitive soul to the act of sensing, a liaison is already noted with the superior faculty of judging, which is rational.

But common sense is not a sixth sense, and on this point Averroes again takes up Aristotle's arguments. If there were a sixth sense, it would correspond to sense objects other than those that we know. It would have its own organ. Sense objects do not reach the senses except through a milieu—water or air—to which the constitution of the corresponding organ should be identical. "But there is no milieu other than water and air, since the earth cannot be a milieu by reason of its hardness, nor can fire, in which nothing can survive. Consequently, it is impossible that a sixth sense exists." The argument, which is Aristotle's, is of course not convincing: if, given the existence of only two milieux, there are already five senses, why could there not be a sixth? For Averroes, moreover, the most solid proof is that if we had a sixth sense, we would apprehend other sense objects than those which are in fact given to us, which is not the case. However, this leaves no way of proving that these other sense objects do not exist outside us. Now, for Averroes, as for Aristotle, all knowledge stems from sensory data. There is consequently a presupposition in the data: the five senses should suffice to cover the totality of sense objects, so that the knowledge based on them can be extended to the totality of what is knowable, which is knowable precisely only coming through them. Consequently, all knowledge that claims to stem from a source other than the five senses is radically eliminated by Averroes, and in this sense he is faithful to the fundamental conception of Aristotle's philosophy.

The imagination

The problems posed by the imagination are what Aristotle examines in his "Treatise on the Soul": Is the imagination the sensitive faculty itself, or the faculty of opinion (*quwwat al-zinn*), or a combination of the two?

The imagination is different from the sensitive faculty; if they act in accord with one another, apprehending one sense object as well as another, they differ in the sense that the imagination applies to sense objects after they have disappeared; it is also more perfect when the senses are at rest, and during sleep. "On the other hand, when the act of sensing (*ihsās*) takes place, the imagination barely seems to exist. If it does appear, it can be distinguished from sensation only with great difficulty. This is why it is thought not to exist in a number of animals, like worms, flies, and mollusks, since we see that these creatures only move when the sense objects appear." The imagination taken by itself can lead us into error, while the sensation that grasps its appropriate sense object is true. "This is why we call imaginations deceptive sense objects." Averroes also points out that the imagination allows us to make up things that we have not sensed, like the phoenix, which has no existence outside the soul. It appears that the creative action of this imagination is specific to man.

The difference between the imagination and opinion is that we can imagine a thing without knowing if it is true or false, while opinion begins with a judgment of veracity (*tasdīq*) or falseness (*takdhīb*). Consequently, being different from sensation and opinion, it is impossible for the imagination to be a combination of the two, since "if the combination is not a confusion, it must necessarily be that it preserves the specific characteristics of each of the components."

Furthermore, the imagination is not an intellect (*ʿaql*), since most of the time we judge veracity at the level of objects of intellect (*maʿqūlāt*), and we pronounce judgments false at the level of imagination. There is a difference between a representation connected to the images of language (*tasawwur nutqī*) and a representation connected to the intellect (*tasawwur ʿaqlī*):

outside all judgment, we picture imaginary representations as being individual and material: "So we would never be able to imagine a color without breadth, even if it is of an order superior to the idea of individuality." Rational representation is the abstraction of the universal idea drawn from matter, not by preserving in its essence a relationship to an individual matter, as is the case for imagination, but by referring back to individuals insofar as they depend on the universal. In this sense, the universal is multiplied with the multiplication of individuals.

The sensible faculty is by nature prior to the imagination. Its relationship to the imagination is what the nutritive faculty is to sensation. It is thus definitely the nutritive soul that is the foundation of imagination in the animal known as man. "The acts of sensing are not the subjects of the imaginative disposition, in the way that we say that the nutritive soul is the subject of the sensible soul." They are the driving forces of the imagination, which gives them their perfection. Some animals can have sensations in actuality without any disposition toward imagining, since they do not sense that they are sensing. If man imagines, it is because his vegetative (nutritive) soul is different from that of the animals, just as it is from that of the vegetables. In effect, it is this soul that is the first entelechy of a body endowed with organs. But it is not the same for all living beings. Since the second entelechies depend on it, they will end up being like it. If man is a reasonable animal, it is because as an animal he is capable of receiving reason: he differs from the other animals by his very animalness itself. Thus, here again we confirm the unity of the human soul in the continuity of its functions, from the nutritive faculty to the imagination. Here we see a development of the first entelechy through a succession of faculties that are first common to all living beings, and then present in the animals and man, and finally exclusively pertinent to man.

The rational faculty

Averroes recalls that the study of a thing begins with the question of its existence (*an sit*), then of its essence (*quid sit*) and its constituents, which are the essential concomitants and the accidents. This research must thus be done regarding the rational faculty. The question of its existence is linked to that of its relationships with the faculties that precede it; then there is the question of knowing if it is sometimes in potentiality, sometimes in actuality, or if it is perpetually in actuality, as many think, even though, "because it is immersed in humidity," it might be retarded in the child; or if it is partially in potentiality and partially in actuality. These are the points upon which the Ancients differed. That being said, Averroes, through his critical examination of the different teachings, was in search of the appropriate answers, taking his inspiration from Aristotle (*De Anima*, 429a10 ff.).

The ideas that the soul apprehends are of two kinds: universal and individual. At the highest point they are distinct, the first being abstracted from matter, and the second apprehended in matter. This being the case, the faculties that apprehend them are necessarily separate. "Now the sensations and the imagination apprehend ideas in matter, even though their reception is not material." There thus exists a separate faculty which apprehends abstract ideas.

However, the role of the rational faculty does not stop there: after apprehending immaterial ideas, it puts them together: we should therefore distinguish between conceptual representation and judgment, although they both come from the same rational faculty, so that there exists no other beyond sensation and imagination. It is moreover this same faculty that gives the principles of knowledge and the principles of action, with the result that a speculative intellect and a practical intellect can be distinguished according to the nature of what is apprehended: either possible ideas relative to the operations of art (moral or other), or necessary ideas whose existence does not depend on our free choice (*ikhtiyār*).

The practical rational faculty. Averroes begins by speaking about the practical faculty. It is, he says, the easiest to study, and it raises few disagreements. It is common to all men; no one is deprived of it. Men differ only in the sense of having more or less of it, while the speculative faculty, in contrast, appears to be completely divine (*ilāhiyya*): it exists only in some men. Most of the practical objects of intellect come to us only through experience (*tajriba*), which relies first on sensation, and then on imagination. They appear and disappear with sensation and perception. In fact, in contrast to the speculative objects of intellect, which have their end in themselves, the practical objects of intellect are concerned with ordering the action that takes place in the world of sense perception and imagination. Hence the question of knowing if imaginary objects are the substrate of or the forces behind the practical rational faculty. Now they are not its substrate, because the universal, as the object of intellect itself, is of another order. Thus, they are the driving force, although not purely and simply, but to the extent that there is in the imagination a disposition toward the universal that distinguishes the human imaginative soul from the animal imaginative soul. Consequently, in man, imaginary objects actualize this disposition and are the driving forces behind the practical rational faculty. The practical objects of intellect thus always exist in relation to the imaginary objects, and this permits reasonable action to be carried out in the world of perceptions and experience.

It follows that practical objects of intellect do not present themselves as eternal truths to be contemplated through speculative knowledge, but that they are "generable and corruptible." They appear to men only in concrete situations, apprehended by the imagination, which then sets the rational faculty into motion by actualizing the universal disposition through forms upon which the existence of objects of practical activity (*al-umur al-masnūʿa*) depend. Under these conditions Averroes can conclude: "If these practical objects of intellect existed without the imaginative soul, their existence would be vain and useless." Bees undoubtedly know how to build hexagonal cells, and spiders weave their webs. But the difference comes from the fact that these tasks among the animals are the work of nature, while in man they come from thought (*fikr*) and invention (*istinbāt*), which belong to the domain of the rational faculty.

Through this faculty, man loves and hates, lives in society and forms friendships. It is the source of moral virtues, "for the existence of these virtues is nothing more than that of the imaginations through which we are moved to practice virtuous acts in the most appropriate manner, with courage where courage is called for, with temperance where temperance is needed, and at the right moment." The data of imagination are apprehended with reflection and deliberation. What seems to be a virtue among the animals comes, on the contrary, from nature.

The speculative rational faculty. Teachings about this faculty differ considerably, and the Peripatetics, in particular, disagree with Plato. The first point to clarify is that of knowing if the speculative objects of intellect are always in actuality—as Ideas are in the intelligible domain (τόπος νοητός) for the Platonists— or if they are first in potentiality, in which case they would, in a certain sense, be material. The question comes down to one of knowing how objects of intellect, which can be nothing more than pure forms, come to us. "Is it, as they say, that the active intellect joins us at the moment of their acquisition?" From this point of view, "in us, they are in the same situation we are when we find ourselves being kept from apprehending them; but when the subject capable of receiving them according to the final disposition arrives on the scene, they appear and are apprehended." Consequently, so that the objects of intellect can be present to us, they have no need of an intelligible driving force, of an intellect that makes them pass from potentiality into actuality. It is just like the rust example: that which makes it disappear from a mirror is in one sense the same cause that draws images on the mirror. In other words, the active intellect is not the driving force that would make objects of intellect in potentiality pass into actuality; its action acts, not on objects of intellect, but on the human faculty capable of receiving them. That which is in potentiality is our faculty of receiving them. What this potentiality is remains to be known.

Averroes then remarks that material forms (the form of the human being, for example) are compound in themselves: they entail something that is in them like a form, which can be extracted from matter, and something that is like matter, which makes it exist for a material being, and which abstraction cannot hold back. In fact, there is a double abstraction, one in relation to exterior matter, and the other in relation to the material side of the material form. This is why the object of intellect of material forms has no existence outside the intelligence that understands them by abstracting them according to this double abstraction. It is quite clear at the level of concepts, and this is foundational to the conceptualist doctrine as opposed to the Platonic realism of Ideas, which supposes that they can be directly shared by material things.

Objects of intellect have a number of characteristics whose existence distinguishes them from psychic forms (*al-suwar al-nafsāniyya*). They are neither generable nor corruptible, but this is not enough for them to be considered immaterial. Actually, the sky has a matter, and this matter is unengendered and incorruptible. We must therefore examine whether or not there is an object of intellect characterized by that which is particular to separate things, and, in the case that such an object of intellect does not exist, whether or not objects of intellect exist with the general characteristics of material things.

Averroes wrote: "It can appear, as far as the existence of intelligible forms is concerned, that for man they are distinct from the other psychic forms that are in him, since the latter forms are found in the subject that can be pointed to with the finger (*al-mushār ilayhi*) outside him, and their existence is something other than that of the object of intellect within him: they are one insofar as they are understood, but multiple insofar as they are individual in matter. As for the forms of objects of intellect, it might be thought that their intelligible existence is their existence itself apprehended objectively, although the object of intellect in them is something other than that which exists [in the object]." In other words, when we think an abstract concept, it is in the soul that thinks it with respect to material realities, for example, our concept of man with respect to men in existence, because, according to Aristotle, there is no thought without image (οὐκ ἔστι νόησις ἄνευ φαντάσματος). A concept no longer exists outside of us when we cease to think it in order to think another. The unity of the concept, for us, encompasses a relationship to a plurality of things in matter. But, as an object of intellect, although the concept may be in the soul that is thinking it, it could have an existence in itself, as an object of thought, and the question is one of knowing whether, in this sense, the object of intellect can be separate. Whence the alternative: if the intelligible side of these forms in us has no existence in itself, they are generable and corruptible along with that of which they are formed, and if their intelligible form has its own existence, they will be separate, or at least there will be something in them which is separable. But whatever the case may be, nothing proves absolutely that human thought, when it apprehends a concept abstractly, affects an object of intellect which, thus abstracted, would exist separately in itself. It could still keep some relationship to matter.

In thought, what distinguishes objects of intellect from the other psychic forms is that, given that they are universal, their apprehension has no limit, in contrast to the knowledge of a particular whose existence is limited in space and time. It can thus be thought that from this point of view they are fundamentally immaterial. Nevertheless, Averroes remarks, universality is here again insufficient to guarantee total separation. And on this point he distinguishes between conceptual representation, which is due to the rational faculty, and judgment due to this same faculty, "for they are two distinct acts." Conceptualization undoubtedly consists in abstracting concepts from the material multiplicity of individuals, but if, in so doing, it suppresses that multiplicity, this does not absolutely entail the expression of all multiplicity. Actually, in concepts, forms are abstracted from a defined multiplicity, for example, the multiplicity of men, but they enter into a judgment bearing on an undefined multiplicity [all men without exception]; "it must thus necessarily be that such an act [of judgment] belongs to an immaterial faculty." Now, judging something is apprehending it. Consequently, "it appears that this faculty, which is in us, is immaterial." Nevertheless, Averroes here qualifies his statement again, for he says, "It is not yet evident that this judgment bears on the universal objects of intellect; it might be that it belongs to the domain of another faculty which, with respect to these objects of intellect, could serve as form." This qualification by Averroes is important: it could be that the judgment "all men are mortal" is not the apprehension of the universality of the concept of man, but rather only the logical form of this concept. Thus, although the activity of logical thought may be an activity of reason, it is not necessarily guaranteed that it apprehends the reality of objects of intellect as such. The result is that logic, which is only formal, cannot be taken as a basis for metaphysical research into the real nature of the rational faculty.

What characterizes the apprehension of the intellect is that in it the apprehension is itself what is apprehended: the intellect is the object of intellect itself. Here Averroes is using an idea that goes back to Neoplatonism, and which was taken up by Fārābī and Avicenna. But for these thinkers, it was a question of the Intellect located on the second level of the cosmic emanation. Averroes applies it to the intellect in general, and to the rational faculty of man in particular. Here he is undoubtedly thinking about the idea of Avempace (whom he knew well), for whom, in a third kind of knowledge, the human intellect apprehends not only objects of intellect, but the intelligibility of these objects of intellect, meaning itself. He writes: "The cause of this is that in abstracting from matter the intelligible forms of things, and in receiving them in an immaterial fashion, it happens that the intellect understands itself, since the objects of intellect, to the extent that it understands them, do not come into it in a form distinct from that which they have in things exterior to the soul." It is in this that the intellect differs from the senses, which do not receive the sense objects drawn from matter such as they are in things outside the soul. There is, between the sensible substance in things and the sensation that apprehends it, an intermediary, which is the material organ. But there is no such intermediary between the intellect and objects of intellect outside the soul. This is why it identifies with them, since there is no separation between it and them. Consequently, the apprehension of objects of intellect is never passive, as is the apprehension of sense objects. Also, one of the characteristics of the intellect in man is that it grows with age, in contrast to the other faculties of the soul. Avicenna had emphasized this fact to prove the incorporeity of the intellect. Moreover, by way of example, when we have looked at a strongly lighted object, we are then unable to see an object in weaker light. A very strong sensation weakens the sensible faculty. Such is not the case with the intellect, which becomes stronger with exercise, and which, moreover, can understand several things at a time, whereas one sensation must stop in order to be replaced by another.

When we look at these characteristics specific to the objects of intellect, it appears that the cause is that the objects of intellect are, as such, denuded of all relationship to individuals, in contrast to the objects of the other faculties of the soul. When we wish to prove that the existence of the objects of intellect is in actuality pure and perpetual, we commit an error of logic: the proposition that all that is perpetually in actuality is necessarily denuded of all individual relation is not convertible, and it cannot be concluded that all that is denuded of such a relationship exists perpetually in actuality. In fact, objects of intellect come and go in human thought, since it is not always thinking intellectually.

This being the case, when we examine how objects of intellect come to us, particularly those which respond to a previous experience (*tajriba*), it appears as though we should first pass through sensation, then through imagination. It is then possible for us to apprehend the universal. This is why he who is missing a sense is deprived of an object of intellect, just as he who does not perceive the individuals of a species will never apprehend their object of intellect, "as in the case of the elephant for us [in Spain]." Moreover, these two faculties need the memory. It is through repetition of the act of sensing that the universal is imbedded in us. This is why these objects of intellect come to us only in time. It is very important to note that Averroes is underscoring here the role of memory.

It seems that this may also be the case for another kind of objects of intellect, about which we know neither when nor how they have come to us. "When we first apprehend the individuals that correspond to them, we do not remember when we first happened to apprehend them in the situation that is present to us in experience [. . .]. These are not a different kind of objects of intellect that are separated from experience; so it must be that they [all] come to us in a unique manner." Averroes is here referring to the principles of what is known as *a priori* knowledge which, as such, seem not to be drawn from experience, like other objects of intellect. In reality, "the existence of these objects of intellect follows a change (*taghayyur*) in what exists in sensation and imagination in an essential way [. . .]. Otherwise, it would be possible for us to understand several things without having sensual perception of them." This rejection of innate *a priori* rational principles and the explanation given for it are reminiscent of a debate that takes the same tack in Ibn Hazm of Cordoba's *Fisal,* which Averroes could have known: if three dates are given to a small child, he cries if one is taken away. His tears follow a change in his perceptions, which awakens in him, without his even being able to put it into words, the principle that the whole is greater than the part. If he is sitting on his mother's lap and he is taken off, this change makes him weep, since he sees that a body cannot be located in two different places at the same time. This is how principles that claim to be called *a priori* boil down to a certain rational manner of reacting to modifications in sense experience, and this is why Averroes rejects the Platonic theory that explains knowledge through remembering. If we have forgotten the moment that we acquired the knowledge of a certain kind of objects of intellect, this does not imply that we cannot know them in some way other than the recollection outlined in the *Meno*. This point of view of Plato's "makes vain the learning of wisdom (*taʿallum al-hikma*): it does not hold up."

It is evident that if we had a constant and unwavering sensation or imagination, our knowledge would not progress, and we would not have access to the objects of intellect. It is changes at this level that stimulate the apprehension of a universal. There is thus, between universal concepts and the specific imaginations of individual changing beings that are dependent on them, a relationship (*idāfa*) by virtue of which the universal becomes existent, for it has no existence, except in that it is universal for particular individuals. This is similar to the relationship of a father and son who are related to each other. They exist together in potentiality or in actuality. When one exists, the other exists; when one disappears, the other disappears. One of the individuals existing outside the soul can undoubtedly survive when the other disappears; but the father, for example, is no longer a father when he no longer has a son, and he becomes a father as soon as he has a son. This is the way relatives appear when looked at either in potentiality or in actuality. "It might be possible for these universal concepts not to rely on the imagination of their subjects, if they existed in actuality outside the soul, as Plato wished. But it is clear that universal concepts have no existence outside the soul." What exists outside the soul, for these objects of intellect, is purely and simply nothing more than their individuals (*ashrās*).

Let us note that the strength of the argument insists that the relationship called *idāfa* is the name given to a category, and that it has an ontological meaning, while the rapport called *nisba* has only logical value. Actually, a *nisba* is a rapport established between two objects that exist independently of it; so when two existing men are taken separately, it can be said that one is the father and the other is the son. Now one of them can die and the other survive. *Idāfa*, on the other hand, is the relationship that constitutes the quality of its two terms. Consequently, if, as in Plato, one had Ideas on the one hand and individuals on the other, a rapport, a *nisba*, could be established between them—a rapport of participation, for example—but the individuals could disappear without the Ideas being touched. Such is not the same with the relationship, the *idāfa*, between the concept and the imagination of its individuals: they exist together, either in actuality, or in potentiality, and they disappear together. There is thus a real constitutive relationship between the universal concept and the imagination of its individuals.

It follows from this that the object of intellect of the man whom Aristotle is thinking is different from that of the man whom

Averroes is thinking, because each of them is in relationship to a different imagination. These concepts, which in one sense are singular, multiply with the number of their subjects. "This connection of objects of intellect with the forms of the imagination entails, for them, their being forgotten when the forms disappear and, for us, fatigue when we think about them: their apprehension by him whose imagination has gone bad is disrupted." If universal objects of intellect were not multiplied by the multiplicity of individual imaginations, untenable absurdities would result, including "that every object of intellect produced in me would be produced in you; that when I learn a science, you would learn it; that when I forget it, you would forget it." What is more, there would be, then, absolutely no acquisition, nor any forgetting of the science. All of Aristotle's sciences would exist in actuality for people who have not yet read his books. The patent falseness of such consequences clearly shows that objects of intellect follow changes in experience, that they multiply with their subjects—but in the imagination, and not in things—just as the forms of individuals that have matter multiply.

In fact, the human intellect does not understand constantly. It thus passes from potentiality into actuality, like the objects of intellect that it understands. Now, whoever says "potentiality" says "matter." But here, "matter" is said in a "figurative and metaphorical" sense. It is taken as the most appropriate cause of contingency in a being (*hudūth*). Thus, there is, in man, a disposition that makes him capable of imagining objects of intellect and apprehending them. But in contrast to a true material disposition (*istiʿdād hayūlānī haqīqī*), this disposition does not belong to these objects of intellect, as if it constituted them before we received them. It is also possible for us to think of this disposition as contingent and the objects of intellect that it allows us to receive as eternal (*azaliyya*). It is thus clear that the faculty that has, in us, the tendency to receive objects of intellect, is in potentiality without being really material in the proper sense of the word "matter": its materiality means nothing other than the simple fact that it is not always in actuality. This detail is important metaphysically, since it supposes a certain independence of the human intellect relative to the materiality of the organic body, but it does not say exactly what the mode of being of this faculty in potentiality is. And that is the whole question.

Themistius and certain early commentators thought that this faculty, which they called the material intellect, was eternal, while the objects of intellect that existed in it were generable and corruptible by virtue of the fact that they were tied to the forms of the imagination. Other commentators, among them Avicenna, contradicted themselves, without being aware of it, by admitting that objects of intellect were eternal while occurring to us in a contingent fashion, and that they have an eternal matter, because they are in potentiality at some times and in actuality at others. That is the contradiction, for what is in potentiality and then in actuality could not be eternal, but rather occurs necessarily, unless, as we have said, what is meant by potentiality is that the objects of intellect are plunged into humidity in us and thus kept from being understood, without ceasing to exist. Averroes then says that they have matter, but in a metaphorical sense. On the other hand, those who hold this thesis mean to speak of true matter. But can the conditions of such matter be applied to the objects of intellect? Certainly not.

The problem comes from the fact that man is not always thinking. It can thus be said that, when he thinks the objects of intellect in actuality, they are for him in potentiality when he is not thinking them. But this potentiality does not affect the objects of intellect themselves. Should the object of intellect in itself not thus be distinguished from the object of intellect in human thought? When a man is conceived, he passes from potentiality into actuality, but his intelligible form itself is not affected by such an event. Otherwise, his form would also need to be conceived out of what would be his being in potentiality. Aristotle has actually well noted that what is conceived is neither matter nor form, but the combination of matter and form. Thus, in nature, forms exist only in generable and corruptible beings, it is in them and through them that they occur, but in themselves they remain immutable. When the human intellect, through abstraction, apprehends them as objects of intellect, it consequently apprehends them in actuality as objects of intellect, that is, not generable and not corruptible. The act of abstracting does not cause them to pass from what would be their being in potentiality to their being in actuality. That goes without saying, since abstraction apprehends precisely that which is and does not occur.

Besides, what would this matter be in intelligible forms? It could not be, as we have just seen, a tendency to pass into actuality. Would it then be a tendency to make them receivable by thought as objects of intellect? But that would make no more sense than saying that there is in sensible forms a disposition to make them perceptible to the senses. Saying that the sense objects are perceptible is saying that the faculty of sensation can understand them. Likewise, objects of intellect are accessible to thought, not because they have a disposition to be received, but because there is in thought a faculty capable of receiving them. A disposition needs a subject, and in the present case the subject of the disposition to be understood in actuality could not be the object of intellect itself, or else every object of intellect would be apprehended, and there would be no more adventitious intelligible knowledge, which is contradicted by the facts. The question is thus one of knowing why the objects of intellect are not always understood. It is as Averroes said on a number of occasions, because there is an impediment. Now such an impediment cannot have originated from the objects of intellect themselves, which would mean that the objects of intellect have the power to obstruct their own understanding, which would be absurd. What, then, is the impediment, and what can suppress it? In other words, where is this potentiality that explains the discontinuity of rational thought, passing from potentiality to actuality and re-becoming in potentiality, since it is not the object of intellect itself?

Themistius notes that if one's gaze had a color, the color would keep it from seeing the other colors. Similarly, there cannot be in the material intellect any of the forms that will then be found there in actuality; otherwise, it would get in the way of the reception of all the others. But concerning this matter—relative to the so-called material intellect—in which the disposition to receive all objects of intellect is said to exist, Averroes asks: Is it something in actuality or not? The question cannot be avoided, since, as we have seen, any disposition to produce that which occurs needs an existent subject, which is necessarily in actuality. Just as the subject in which no actuality of any kind exists is the prime matter (which, by the way, has no separate existence), and because one cannot suppose that prime matter is what receives these objects of intellect—since on the other hand this subject should be something in actuality in order for it to be the subject of a disposition—is it an acceptable solution to say with Themistius that this is a question of intellect?

In reply, Averroes notes that if the material subject that receives the objects of intellect is an intellect, "it is, existing in actuality, of the same genus as that for which it is in potentiality, which is absurd, because potentiality and actuality are contradictory." In fact, if it is in actuality, it understands in actuality objects of intellect for which it is in potentiality.

For Averroes, it is consequently the soul, and not an intellect, which is necessarily the subject of the disposition in question, "for a thing in potentiality has, through itself, nothing in actuality of that for which it is in potentiality." So if the subject is a soul, "of all the faculties of the soul, there is nothing closer to the requirement of being the subject of these objects of intellect than the forms of the imagination, since we have seen that objects of intellect exist only in connection to them, that they exist when the forms of the imagination exist, and they disappear when [the forms] disappear." Consequently, the disposition to receive objects of intellect, which is in the forms of the imagination, is the first material intellect (*al-ʿaql al-hayūlānī al-awwal*). It marks the continuity between the imagination and intellection. Now what is imagined means what is understood. But this first material intellect, as a disposition of the imagination, should receive itself while receiving the objects of intellect that correspond to its disposition. This is why it appears that the intellect in potentiality should be something else, a second material intellect. But what is it? Might it not be what the first material intellect becomes when it receives objects of intellect? Here we come upon a very important passage in Averroes' paraphrase, one whose text we will closely examine.

As Aristotle said, "it is perhaps a substance that is all the objects of intellect in potentiality, without being in itself anything whatsoever, for a thing in itself could not be able to understand the totality of things [. . .]." It consequently seems, in the case of objects of intellect, that they may be linked to two subjects: the first, eternal, in which they all are; and the second, which belongs to man, generable and corruptible, that is to say, the forms of the imagination. The intellect *in habitu* (*al-ʿaql bi'l-malaka*) is made up of objects of intellect that come into actuality in this subject that receives them when man wishes to have a representation of them. Such is the case for the learned man when he does not exercise his knowledge [. . .]. Thus linked to the disposition of the imagination, that is, to the first material intellect, the intellect *in habitu* is corruptible.

"Through this disposition, which exists in man in the forms of the imagination, what he imagines is distinguished in itself from what animals imagine." This means that what he imagines is intelligible in potentiality by virtue of this disposition specific to man. "But [. . .] the disposition to receive objects of intellect that is in the forms of the imagination receives these objects of intellect without their being mixed with the forms, for if there were such mixing, it would no longer be possible to understand the forms of the imagination, just as it would not be able to receive color if the sense of sight had a color. It is in this sense that it has been said that if the material intellect had a particular form, it would not be able to receive forms." This texts requires some clarification. When, for example, we have an image of a man, it is intelligible in potentiality because it has in the imagination a disposition to become intelligible. It is in this sense that Aristotle said: I see the man in Callias, where an animal would see only Callias. But this disposition to receive objects of intellect is that of the imagination taken as a faculty of imagining all possible forms, not taken as it imagines one form or another like the image of the man in our example. If the object of intellect "man" were mixed with the image of Callias so that it was a constitutive element, I would no longer see the man in Callias, but I would apprehend only the man-Callias next to the man-

Socrates, without making the distinction between what is the man in Callias and the man in Socrates, that is, without seeing the man in Callias and in Socrates. An image can thus accompany the thought of an intelligible concept: ουκ εστι νόησις ἄνευ φαντάσματος, but it cannot be [an intelligible concept's] constitutive element. It is the disposition specific to the faculty of imagining, that is, the material intellect, which receives it, at the time of an image, certainly, but without keeping anything of it.

Beyond this, it would seem that the imagination, through the disposition that it has in itself, would be more entitled to be a driving force of the material intellect than to be the receptor of objects of intellect. This is why Alexander says that the material intellect is purely and simply a disposition to the exclusion of forms [of the imagination]. He meant that there is no form that is a condition of the reception of objects of intellect by the intellect. The disposition of the imagination, in man, would then be the condition of the existence of the material intellect, but not by virtue of the fact that it receives in actuality objects of intellect that are in potentiality in the imagination. This interpretation, however, poses a problem, because the material intellect, thus considered, is nothing as long as it does not receive objects of intellect: it is then nothing more than a simple disposition of the imagination that is undoubtedly an indispensable condition of its existence, but that cannot pass into actuality by itself. This would assume that objects of intellect in potentiality in images pass into actuality by themselves. The result would be that the possibility of existence of the material intellect would be based in the imagination, but that its existence in actuality, which implies that it understands, would be due to a driving force that is not the imagination. How can this be conceived? Should the material intellect be thought of as being outside the soul? We already know that this is not the way Averroes thinks of it. Let us take a look at what he said about the matter.

In order to understand the conclusion that his critique would reach, we must closely examine what is in potentiality and what passes into actuality. On the one hand, objects of intellect are in potentiality in the forms of the imagination; on the other, the material intellect is in potentiality in the disposition of the human imagination. The objects of intellect only pass into actuality at the moment that the material intellect itself passes into actuality and understands by receiving these objects of intellect in actuality. And for this it needs a mover in actuality, as is generally the case for any being in potentiality that passes into actuality. It needs a mover that can be neither the objects of intellect that are in potentiality in the imagination, nor the disposition which, as such, is not in actuality, even though it belongs to the existing subject that is man's imagination.

We are thus led to the conclusion that there is an intellect in actuality, distinct from the material intellect: "As the mover in fact gives to what it moves that which is its substance, it is equally necessary that it be an intellect and that it be, moreover, absolutely immaterial: the material intellect, as such, necessarily has need in its existence for there to be an intellect existing perpetually in actuality, without which it would not exist." Consequently, this active intellect is nobler than the material intellect. "It exists in itself in actuality like a perpetual intellect, whether we think it or not, and it is in every respect identical to that which it understands; it is a form and it is active [. . .]. This is why it can be considered possible for us to understand the material intellect in a future life (*bi-ākhira*), that is, insofar as it is a form for us that necessarily comes to us like an eternal object of intellect. It is in itself an intellect, whether we think it or not." It is not like the material objects of intellect that come out of our act of abstraction. It is intelligible for us by virtue of what we call "union" and "conjunction" (*bi'l-ittiḥād wa'l-ittiṣāl*). However, this possibility of a life after death, as it is presented in this context, is not yet that of a personal immortality. Alexander thought that what Aristotle meant by acquired intellect (*al-ʿaql al-mustafād*) was the active intellect in so far as this conjunction with us exists for it: hence its name, which means that we acquire it.

The theory of the active intellect was illustrated especially by Avempace, who dedicated a treatise to it, one to which Averroes did not remain indifferent. But let us see whether this conjunction is possible for man, or not.

In order to answer this question, "the philosophers rely on the fact that the speculative intellect (*al-ʿaql al-naẓarī*), in naturally isolating the forms from their subjects, isolates a non-separate form that is not in itself an intellect; it should thus, *a fortiori*, isolate the separable form that is in itself an intellect." In other words, this intellect isolates by abstraction an intelligible concept, but it is clear that this concept is not an object of intellect at the highest point of its intelligible perfection. It remains linked to the contingency of experiences. For man, the final perfection and the ultimate goal is that of arriving at perfectly separate objects of intellect which, having absolutely no relationship to matter, are an intellect. For Avempace, the Blessed (*al-Suʿadāʾ*) are men whose knowledge, beyond the abstract knowledge of the learned, reaches the intelligibility of the objects of intellect, that is, the intelligibility of the Intellect itself. It is in this that conjunction consists. But if we follow closely what Aristotle says, what is most evident, according to Averroes, is that it is not possible for the material intellect to enter into conjunction with the active intellect, since then it would be a substance that would receive a faculty in actuality from which it would draw the objects of intellect; but in this case, it would have a form and it could no longer receive all the forms. Now such is not the same case with the relationship of the imagination to the material intellect. "Regarding the imagination, its relationship to the material intellect is that of the sense object to the sense, for example of what is visible to sight, not of the eye to sight." This means that the imagination is not a subject relative to the material intellect, but, as we have seen, a subject relative to the tendency that is in the imagination. Consequently, for Averroes the material intellect is not such that it can receive the objects of intellect—insofar as they are purely objects of intellect—directly from the active intellect, without owing anything to the imagination. His objection is that then, existing in actuality, it would have a form that would keep it from apprehending all other forms. Averroes declared that he was definitely misled by Avempace's teaching.

Here is the short summary Averroes offered: "There are two kinds of men: the blessed and the common men of humanity. It is not possible for what two common men understand to be, numerically, one single object of intellect, for this would give rise to a number of absurdities"; for example, "that man existed before his existence and that knowledge is a recollection [reminiscent of the thesis of a vision of Ideas before birth as maintained in the myth of Plato's *Meno*]; that learning according to the natural course of things is not qualitative, but quantitative, so that all objects of intellect existing in actuality for Aristotle could be found as such for anyone else whosoever." In other words, what would make the difference among men in what they think would be reduced to a greater or lesser difference in the number or the clarity of the thoughts they remember. Averroes had already considered this criticism and showed that a single object of intellect multiplies numerically in such men "because the spiritual forms (*al-suwar al-rūhāniyya*) are multiplied by the multiplication of individuals."

As for the blessed who are at the height of their final perfection, they are in a contrasting situation: "It is impossible to find among men two examples of a blessed man, both of whom are considered to be so in their final perfection. For if we suppose that blessedness consists of the intellect, which is in actuality, and which *in habitu* has reached its final perfection, while it has been explained that this intellect is multiplied by the multiplication of persons, and if we introduce two blessed men according to the qualification of blessedness so defined, it will necessarily result that in each of them the intellect of the one and that of the other will have the same, single object of intellect. [. . .] If the object of intellect of one of the two blessed men is different from the object of intellect in the other, it will be necessary for these two objects of intellect to have a single object of intellect in each of them." [. . .] Whatever the case, "The representation of the blessed men will necessarily need to end up with a representation that is single in number from all points of view, without the slightest multiplicity." However, it is impossible to go to infinity; otherwise, final perfection would not exist: in fact, it is characteristic of it to be a pure actuality where there is absolutely no potentiality, neither beginning nor end. "Consequently, it clearly appears that the faculty of representation which is the faculty of this intellect and the representation that is *in habitu* are simply homonyms." That is, there is nothing in common between the abstract apprehension of objects of intellect in the intelligence of the common people, and even of the learned, and the final, perfect apprehension of the intelligibility of the intellect.

From this point of view, then, intellects in actuality and *in habitu* of common men and of the learned apprehend abstract objects of intellect that differ from one individual to another, and they are thus not perfectly intelligible. But these intellects do not reach the point of perfection, except when they apprehend a single, pure object of intellect. It appears that we are not betraying Avempace in what Averroes reports, when we say that the plurality of the blessed (*al-suʿadāʾ* is a plural) is in harmony with the road traveled to arrive at final perfection, since what makes a person blessed is the actual attainment of intellectual perfection.

But Avempace has another method, which is a demonstrative truth. How does man raise himself up to this perfection? There is a hierarchy of objects of intellect: (1) At the level of the common man are the objects of intellect of vulgar knowledge, which are generable and corruptible, being linked to the imagination; (2) Then come the speculative objects of intellect (*al-maʿqūlāt al-nazariyya*), which also include degrees: first, the mathematical objects of intellect, and then those of the science of nature. The objects of intellect of the common people and those of the learned have in common that they rely on the imagination. The difference is that the common person is turned toward the practical and is interested in objects of intellect with a view toward the individuals that they order, while the learned, on the other hand, consider individuals only in view of their objects of intellect. The objects of intellect of the sciences are diversified in turn, according to the function of objects, sometimes material and sometimes spiritual.

The learned man rises up to a higher level "for he thinks objects of intellect that do not exist among the objects of his learning, and which are separate forms (*al-suwar al-mufāriqa*). He then understands perfectly incorruptible objects of intellect that do not rely on subjects and that have no subjects." Such is the path that Avempace followed to justify the possibility of conjunction with the active intellect.

Averroes then remarks that if the learned man who studies the science of nature raises himself to objects of intellect that are not those of material things (*maʿqūlāt umur hayūlāniyya*), it is without any doubt that he finds them in the science of that which is beyond nature (metaphysics: *ʿilm mā baʿd al-tabīʿa*). "But I would like to know," he says, "if the objects of intellect found in this science are eternal, so that there might be a science that is not first in potentiality, then in actuality." If the objects of intellect of this science are eternal, they do not rely on the forms of the imagination. It appears, however, that the objects of intellect that enter into metaphysics are far from being present here.

It is obvious for whoever considers this science that it represents these separate objects of intellect according to the relationship (*munāsaba*) and analogy (*muqāyasa*) that exist between them and the material objects of intellect, and that it suppresses in the separate objects of intellect the adventitious characteristics that, being material, accompany the objects of intellect. "This is how we say that the intellect and what it understands are from all points of view the exact same thing when it is a question of separate objects of intellect, and that objects of intellect in us are touched by a change from which separate objects of intellect are exempt." In fact, we do not consider their quiddity (*māhiyya*) except on the basis of material objects of intellect, and the science of the soul necessarily precedes metaphysics. "This is why it is said: Know yourself [and] you will know your creator." Let it be noted that this conclusion is in complete conformity with Aristotle's fundamental idea: the physics that studies nature precedes metaphysics, and the soul is a nature. It follows that in man, the soul is at the origin of all knowledge, knowledge of physics, first, of metaphysics next, and, in it, of separate objects of intellect.

In summary, everything metaphysics tells us that relates to separate things is that they have a nobler existence in the sense that the cause is nobler than the effect. This is how metaphysics speaks by analogy about the first intellect as well as about the simplest of all the intellects, as it does about a cause that is absolutely not an effect, outside of which nothing essentially existing can be represented.

If separate objects of intellect are understood according to their similarity to the material objects of intellect, they all fall under the category of relationship (*idāfa*), meaning that they are born and disappear at the same time. Consequently, the representations of metaphysics do not exist perpetually in actuality. They are adventitious for us; we apprehend them only on the basis of material objects contingent to physics, "for they are not the substance (*jawhar*) of these things" that the metaphysician studies, "although they are close to them." In other words, the ideas that man can have of things beyond nature through separate objects of intellect are near to what their reality is, but they are not their substance, in contrast to what Plato teaches. As a result, the metaphysician is in a situation analogous to that of the man "who imagines something by the concomitant characteristics that accompany its substance, when it is impossible for him to imagine the thing itself; these are fundamentally the highest degrees of objects of intellect." They come from the final effort that man makes to know what is beyond nature, that is, beyond sensible experience, which, being that it is what is clearest to him, remains the basis of all knowledge. From common experience to the science of physics, there is a hierarchy through which man progresses, up to the farthest limit of the accomplishments of his thought.

The last question is that of knowing if conjunction with the pure object of intellect, this state in which man reaches his final perfection, is, or is not, a perfection of nature. If it is not natural and is of a different kind, it is divine. But how is it possible for there to exist for a natural being a perfection that is not natural? If it seems as though this final state is not a natural perfection, it is because if it were natural, all other faculties of the soul and material objects of intellect would enter, in a way, into the existence of this perfection, just as everything that is ordered to an end enters the end. Thus, perfection would be material and would exist throughout the existence of these faculties of the soul. "Now that is absurd, or else nature would have worked in vain by preparing things for an end whose property it is to exclude them," since the end of human knowledge is precisely to free itself from materiality.

This being the case, it is clear that conjunction with the Pure Object of Intellect is not a natural perfection for a being of the nature of man. It remains for it to be a perfection in the sense that separate forms are said to be a perfection for celestial bodies endowed with circular movement. In this sense, the human intellect would be attracted toward the pure intellect, as the celestial spheres are toward the immobile mover. In any case, this is a perfection different from the natural perfection specific to the material beings of the sublunar world.

When we think about what man's situation would be in such a conjunction, it appears that it would be one of the marvels of nature (*aʿājīb al-tabīʿa*). It would be the compound of an eternal and a corruptible, analogous to an intermediary between plant and animal, or between animal and man. Now this kind of existence is far from the existence that is specific to man as man.

This is the state to which the Sufis aspire. It is evident that they do not reach it, since one cannot reach it except through speculative knowledge, which they have given up, just as they cast off the senses and the other faculties of the soul. This is how their state appears to them to be a divine perfection. On this point Averroes is in agreement with Avempace in his criticism of the mystics. It is only through homonymy that one can speak of a faculty open to natural perfection and a faculty open to divine perfection. When the faculty for natural perfection exists in actuality, there is entelechy in its relationship to what it perfects. According to this relationship, the active intellect is called acquired. In other words, the active intellect is not for man a separate perfection that he would reach in knowledge of the pure object of intellect in itself, by breaking with all that precedes it in the soul, but it is an act that gives to human knowledge the final perfection of an acquired intellect.

Conclusion

What is the result of this quite detailed and nuanced commentary on the *Treatise on the Soul*? First, Averroes totally repudiates Platonism. There are no separate Ideas; the objects of intellect are apprehended by a human intellect and in it, and their apprehension does not raise it above and beyond itself. If there were in man a pure intellectual thought, a νόησις, to think pure objects of intellect, it would not be anyone's thought, and unicity of intellect for all men could be spoken of. But such is not the case, regardless of what criticism Averroes might have received on this point. If a plurality of men come together as one on a single truth, it is not only through the truth that they lose their identity in a single intellect, it is also that they have progressively perfected their knowledge on the basis of sense perceptions. This is why Averroes is opposed to the Neoplatonism of the Eastern *falāsifa*, Fārābī and Avicenna, and to the idea that the active intellect is, in the cosmic hierarchy, the intellect of the moon, which they identify with the angel Gabriel, and whose function is that of being the giver of forms (*wāhib al-sawar / dator formarum*) to human intellects in the sublunar world. Averroes criticizes their having wanted to reconcile Plato and Aristotle, and he certainly has in mind Fārābī's work entitled *Book on the Agreement of the Opinions of Two Sages*. Nothing proves better the extent to which he is hostile to any doctrine of the separation of objects of intellect or of the intellect.

On the other hand, what does come out of the ensemble of this summary is the conception of the unity of the soul, marked by the continual chain of these different operations, from sensation up to rational thought. This continuity is based on the conviction that man is different from animals, beginning with the nutritive faculty. The soul is undoubtedly the first entelechy of a living body, but this definition does not apply as such to all organized beings. The human body is different, even as a body, from an animal body, and its first entelechy is different from that of the animal body. It is likewise for the second entelechies that follow: the nutritive faculty in man is not identical to what is in an animal, as is the case, also, for the imagination and *a fortiori* for intelligence; this particularity of the human being remains all the way up to the highest functions of his intelligence. The unity of the human soul is the very unity of man, his identity through all the development of his faculties. It is thus in its totality that the human soul gives life to its body, so that it can be said that it is in his living body that man finds the seeds of all his spiritual developments.

What happens after death? Averroes says nothing about this in his commentary except, as has been seen, he does not allow for an immortality that is due to conjunction with an intellect still in actuality, intelligible for man, but which would exist in us whether we understand it or not. He rejects Avicenna's doctrine of conjunction. It is true that Aristotle does not raise this problem, either, although he does say that once it has been separated, the active intellect, taken in its essence, is alone immortal. But if by this we mean the word χωρισθείς as a passive past participle (having been separated), it follows that the separation of the active intellect is the fact of an abstraction of human thought for which it appears in its essence as unengendered and incorruptible, thus as eternal. But, based on the evidence, there is no way for there to be a real conjunction with an abstraction. Consequently, the question of man's survival after death is not explicitly raised by Aristotle, and Averroes has no need to deal with it in his commentary. He would raise the question elsewhere.

CHAPTER IV

Philosopher and Theologian

It is clear that Averroes established himself as a philosopher with his commentaries on Aristotle. We will now look at his works that were not commentaries. These are primarily *The Decisive Treatise, The Book of the Exposition of Demonstrative Methods Relative to the Teachings of Religion,* and especially *The Decay of Decay.*

The Decisive Treatise (Fasl al-maqāl)

What "parentage" (*ittisāl*) is there between Islamic religious law (*sharīʿa*) and wisdom (*hikma*)? That is the question discussed in *The Decisive Treatise.* Let us note the expressions used. Averroes is not speaking about the relationship between faith and reason, or between philosophical truth and dogmatic belief: those are general questions which should be examined under the purview of a single, specific form of research, since a relationship can only exist between works of the same kind. This is why Averroes uses the word "parentage," which has a meaning that is more ontological than logical. For him it is actually not a case of bringing a rational view of things into harmony with a religious view, but of discovering whether or not there is a subjective parentage between the way of life according to the wisdom that philosophy has as its goal, and the way of life according to Religious Law, which is revealed. So it is not from the perspective of an abstract problem that Averroes views the issue, but from the concrete perspective of men who are to live and act in this world. They undoubtedly have a practical mind with which they are able to deliberate and to make decisions. But do they all use it, and, we might add, are they capable of using it well? Averroes' fundamental idea, which is undoubtedly based on daily experience, is that such is not the case. Religious Law is thus in his eyes something that comes to men as an aid to their failing reason. What remains to be shown is that in acting in accord with the Law, they behave according to reason, even though it is not reason that inspires them.

The first question is whether it is permitted, forbidden, commanded, recommended, or, finally, necessary, to look at the Law with a philosophical or logical eye. Setting the necessary aside, since it belongs to the domain of the rational faculty, the prescribed, the forbidden, the recommended (with its counterpart, the discouraged) and the licit are juridical categories (*ahkām*), in the name of which Muslim jurists seek the nature of laws and qualify the acts that depend on them. Consequently, Averroes is not going to examine the Law on the basis of reason, but reason on the basis of what characterizes laws.

Philosophy is nothing more than speculation on beings and on what they express as evidence of a "worker" (*sāniʿ*), since evidence is a product of work (*masnūʿāt*). (We are deliberately translating the Arabic word with the word "worker," in order to underscore that Averroes is not using the Qurʾānic word *khāliq*, creator, here.) "The more perfect the knowledge of the work is, the more perfect the knowledge of the worker will be." This is what philosophy says, independent of all religious revelation.

The Law specifically recommends observing beings and encouraging them to study. It is certain that the Law calls people to such observation, and Averroes cites several verses to show this. The most general is "So observe, you who have eyes to see" (Qurʾān 59:2). This text notes the obligation to use rational reasoning (*qiyās ʿaqlī*), or juridical reasoning (*qiyās sharʿī*), or both at the same time. Let us bear in mind that these two expressions belong to the vocabulary of jurists. Another text he cites is: "Do they not look at the royalty of the heavens and the earth, and what God has created?" (Qurʾān 7:185). This is an encouragement to observe the totality of beings. Since God recommends that men reason in order to prove, it is normal to begin by understanding the different kinds of proof. These considerations lead back to those that we encountered regarding the introduction of logic into juridical research in Averroes' opinion as a jurist. If the Law asks to be studied through *qiyās sharʿī*, one is even more strongly justified in studying it through rational syllogism. Moreover, Averroes notes, most Muslim jurists admit this point of view, with the exception of the "materialists" (*al-hashwiyya*). It is thus permissible for a Muslim to study logic, even if his predecessors in this science were not Muslims themselves.

This last remark is important, for, according to some theologians, those who used sciences whose origin was previous or foreign to Islam were endangering their faith and should be considered infidels. The way Averroes understood it, on the other hand, the Law was quite open; if it was sufficient for common men, it did not isolate them from the learned; a connection remained among all, and communication remained ever possible without the necessity, and far from it, of giving up Qurʾānic revelation. When the Qurʾān invites reflection, it is addressing all men and not only the believers. When one uses the reason to which God refers, and which He gave to man, if a truth is found in what the Ancients said, it should be accepted; if an error is discovered, it should be pointed out. But it is certain that if God recommends seeking the truth, Revelation is not the gift of ready-made scientific knowledge. If He encourages observation of created beings in order to arrive at knowledge of His existence as Creator, this observation can take place on a number of different levels. It is certain that whoever wishes to know the nature of things perfectly and specifically should learn sciences like geometry and astronomy, through which we apprehend the reality of magnitudes and distances. In sum, simple sense perception and imagination may be enough for the common man to persuade himself, if he pays attention, that God exists. But nowhere does the Qurʾān teach that believers should limit themselves to this kind of knowledge.

Besides, the very science of law and its principles (*usūl al-fiqh*), which aims at precise knowledge of the Law, is required by religious Revelation. Considerable time is needed to study the teachings of the doctors of the different schools of law, and to know the questions relative to differences of opinion (*masāʾil al-khilāf*). Here we find the thought of Averroes the jurist on the use of reason in the science of law, particularly to define the application of juridical categories (*ahkām*) and to solve problems raised by harmonizing texts and divisions between schools. It is evident that the common man does not have the leisure to dedicate himself to such study. Nor does God ask this of him: it suffices that he observe the Law such as it is spelled out in the Qurʾān, which reveals its principles, following the opinion of the doctors of the different recognized schools (*madhhāʾib*), when it comes to details and applications. Learned individuals are necessary in the community of the Prophet, but there is no requirement that all the believers be among the learned. This question had been debated by the theologians: does faith imply knowledge or not? They proposed a variety of answers. Averroes' solution is characterized by considerable openness of mind. If faith does not imply knowledge, it does not exclude it; quite the contrary. The goal of faith is the same as that of science.

But rational speculation should not be forbidden to him who is capable of it; that is, to "him who combines the wisdom of thought and a just observation of the Law, as well as moral virtue." Doing so would be "the height of ignorance and straying from God." It can be seen that the problem raised is that of the interior balance of concrete men, and not the conciliation of abstract concepts like reason and faith. The mental shortcomings of some men, or domination by passions, or the fact that they have not found someone to teach them the sciences of the Ancients, should not keep others from gaining access to the knowledge of reason, for damage of this sort happens to men by accident (*biʾl-ʿarad*), and not by essence (*lā biʾl-dhāt*). The bad use that one can make of science does not take precedence over the divine recommendation to study it.

This being the case, Averroes examines the situation where a comparison between the texts of the Qurʾān and the texts of rational wisdom arises. If the Law is silent on such and such question from the realm of philosophy, this is similar to when the *ahkām* are not specified in law and must be deduced by the use of reason. If it is not silent, either the clear meaning of what it says is in agreement with the conclusions of rational proofs, and there is no difficulty, or else it is in disagreement, and it requires a figurative commentary (*taʾwīl*), which consists in "drawing the sense of a word from its proper meaning toward a metaphorical meaning, without thus disturbing the custom of the Arabic language in the use of metaphor, which consists in denoting something by its resemblance to another, or by its cause, or by a consequence, or by a concomitant." We have seen that the jurist uses analogy by resemblance to explicate the Law. Those who practice demonstrative science are permitted to use this means all the more. Here again, we see that the juridical practice serves as a justifying intermediary between knowledge of religious truth and rational knowledge.

All Muslims recognize that there is agreement between the data supplied by reason and the data from tradition (*al-maʿqūl wa'l-manqūl*). But in the Law there are terms which, in their proper sense, support a figurative commentary. All the doctors are not unanimous on the subject of which expressions should be understood metaphorically. This is how the Ashʿarite theologians interpret the verse where it is said that God is seated on a throne, or the hadith revealing that God comes down every night onto the sky of the world, while the Hanbalites take these texts literally. The cause of these differences lies in the disparity of their ways of thinking and in the aptitude for judging that distinguish one man from another. The Qurʾān reserves the use of figurative commentary for believers who are firm in their knowledge: "God has sent down upon you the Book in which there are clear verses, which are the mother of the Book, and ambiguous verses. Those who have a doubt in their heart follow what is ambiguous out of desire to revolt and out of desire to interpret allegorically. But God alone and those who are firm in knowledge know the figurative interpretation" (Qurʾān 3:7). Let us note that Averroes reads the verse in the sense that fits his thesis. But there is another reading which makes God the only subject of the verb, and which links the learned to what follows: God alone knows the *taʾwīl* of these verses, and those who are firm in their knowledge say: We believe. This second reading would run counter to what Averroes is attempting to prove, and would justify the faith of the coal miner.

We are left with the question of knowing what should be taken literally and what should be taken figuratively. Can the consensus of Muslims be relied upon? But this consensus is imposed only in matters of practice, not in questions of theory.

The distinction between theoretical knowledge and practical knowledge is important. There have always been doctors who thought that the religious Laws contained teachings about which all men do not need to have in-depth speculative knowledge. On the other hand, in practical life, no one should be unaware of matters of good and evil, and this knowledge should be revealed to everyone equally. Although the Law specifically addresses the uneducated as well as the learned, the knowledge that it calls for only concerns some men. Averroes here finds a distinction that is common among Islamic thinkers, that of *fard ʿayn*, which is a personal obligation incumbent on every believer, and of *fard kifāya*, "obligation of sufficiency," which is addressed to the Muslim community as such. In order for the latter to be respected, it suffices that a few of the learned—rather than the common faithful—observe it. However, because all of humanity is committed in practical life without any distinction, a consensus on the matter of theoretical and practical knowledge is, in every age, not only possible but required, and it is from this point of view that he who breaks the consensus is accused of infidelity.

However, it is not a question of a breakdown in consensus in those cases where one cannot expect agreement among all the learned, as is the case in figurative commentaries, even when they are indispensible. What can be said, then, about Muslim philosophers like Fārābī and Avicenna, whom Ghazālī calls infidels in his *Tahāfut al-falāsifa* because of their teaching that the world is eternal, and that God does not know details, or when they interpret figuratively the resurrection of the body and the return to God in the life to come (*maʿād*)? Here is the reply: if there is no validity in these matters except in the consensus of those learned who are "firm in their knowledge," and if the teachings of the philosophers do not agree on the matter because they do not know the *taʾwīl*, it is certain that there is no reason justified by the Qurʾān for their teaching to take precedence in questions of faith. In fact, the *falāsifa* deal with questions that are not purely philosophical, but ones in which they are in competition with the learned who are "firm in their knowledge," designated by God to give the explanation. But who are these learned? Are they unquestionably the theologians, and in particular the Ashʿarite theologians whom Ghazālī saw as opposed to the philosophers in his *Tahāfut al-falāsifa*? This was the judgment proffered by the theologians against the philosophers whom Averroes examined and critiqued in his *Tahāfut al-Tahāfut*.

As far as God's knowledge of things is concerned, the peripatetics simply remarked that this knowledge is in no way comparable to ours, since God knows things because He is the cause of their being, whereas we know them as effects. Moreover, for man, universal knowledge is drawn from the nature of the particulars. Consequently God cannot know the particulars through a universal knowledge that is inconceiveable in Him, as it is in us. Thus, God knows neither individual beings nor universal concepts in the way that we do. In this sense, properly speaking, God's knowledge is neither particular nor universal.

A difference of opinion regarding the eternity of the world or its creation pits the Ashʿarite theologians against the philosophers of Antiquity. This difference, especially among some of the Ancients, almost comes down to a difference in names. There are effectively three kinds of beings: two at the extremities of existence and one in the middle. There is agreement on the names for the extremes: at one end are those beings whose existence comes from an efficient cause different from them, comes from matter, and is preceded by time. Such is the case for bodies apprehended through sense perception. The Ancients and the Ashʿarites were in agreement in calling this kind of existence adventitious (*muhdath*). At the other extreme, there is the being that comes from nothing and draws its existence from nothing, and which is not preceded by time. The intermediate species is that of the existent being which comes from nothing, which is not preceded by time, but which owes its existence to an efficient cause: this is the Universe in its totality. If everyone agrees that the existence of the Universe is not preceded by any time whatsoever, and that the time of the world in the future is endless, the divergence comes from the fact that the world's past is considered to be finite. These theologians agree with Plato on this. Aristotle, on the other hand, thinks that the past is infinite, as is the future. The intermediate being, the Universe, is like the superior eternal being in that it is not drawn from anything, and like the inferior temporal being (the sublunar world), subject to generation and corruption, in that it has a cause. For some, its similarity to the superior world is more important, and they call it eternal; for others what matters is its similarity to beings that "happen" in time, and they call it temporarily produced. In reality, it is neither. What is, properly speaking, eternal, is actually without cause, and what is truly produced temporarily is necessarily corruptible. The sky that envelops the Universe is, according to Aristotle, of an incorruptible matter, the "quintessence."

This being said, Averroes concludes that "the teachings concerning the world are not sufficiently far from one another for one of them—but not the others—to be called infidelity." For that, as the theologians think, they would need to be antithetical, but such is not the case. Averroes thus takes the side against the theologians on this point, and the problem of opposition between reason and faith, between rational truth and religious truth, is brought back to the opposition between the theological mind and the philosophical mind.

Moreover, the opinions of theologians regarding the world do not follow the evident meaning of the verses. It appears, from an examination of the texts that speak of the gift of existence (*ījād*) that God gave to His creation, that the form (*sūra*) of the world is really produced in time, that existence and time have a duration both before and after, and are not interrupted. Averroes cites the Qurʾān 11:7: "It is He Who created the heavens and the earth in six days, while His throne was upon the water." But how is such a verse to be understood? In effect, Averroes says, "the evident meaning becomes clear, that is to say that before the existence of the world, there was an existence, that of the throne and of water, and a time before the time of creation, that is, the time connected to the form of this existence, time which is the number of movements of the sphere." We know that for Averroes, as well as for Aristotle, the circular movement of the universe is eternal in the sense that it has neither a point of departure nor a point of arrival, as opposed to rectilinear movement. But the movement of the sphere can be numbered, according to Aristotle's definition that time is the numbered number of movement. It is numbered time which belongs to what the Qurʾān calls the creation in six days. What God creates is the "form" of the world, that is, the order of generable and corruptible existences that appear in the time of the world, an order which is the world itself, the "cosmos"; Averroes thus finds the meaning of the Greek word κόσμος.

Without stopping at all the verses that Averroes cites, let us once again remember this criticism of the theologians: nowhere does the Qurʾān say that "God exists with pure nothingness." If such were the case, creation would be an absolute beginning. But on this point again, the Peripatetic philosophers, in opposition to the theologians, are in agreement with the evident meaning of the Qurʾānic verses.

Averroes then raises the important question of *ijtihād,* the personal effort recommended to Muslim believers for a good understanding of the Law. According to a tradition of the Prophet, "when the judge (*al-ḥākim*) makes an effort and is correct, he receives [from God] two rewards; if he is mistaken, he has only one reward [that of his effort]." But, says Averroes, are there greater judges than those who judge existence, that is, than the learned men charged by the Law to examine difficult questions (*al-masāʾil al-ʿawīsa*)? If they err, they will be excused. But the error of him who is not qualified by the Law is reprehensible, whether it concerns theoretical or practical questions. If such an error pertains to the principles of the Law, it is a mark of the infidelity (*kufr*) of non-Muslims; if it only concerns the consequences of these principles, it is an innovation (*bidʿa*) that authentic faith should reject. The question will undoubtedly arise regarding how we know who is thus qualified. It is certain that for Averroes, the answer is he who is educated and who has studied under the guidance of a competent, recognized, teacher. This guarantee may not be absolute, but it is the only one there is. Let us bear in mind that in Islam there is no body set up to define orthodoxy. Nevertheless, the philosopher of Cordoba had another measure at his disposal: that of scrupulously observing the requirements of Aristotle's demonstrative logic in such a way that the artifices of dialectics—or worse yet, rhetoric—might be avoided. It is of little importance whether the common man manages to recognize the existence of the one God and the mission of the Prophet through ways that are neither justified nor codified by Aristotle. But when it is no longer a question of the very foundations of the faith, but of "hidden things" that can be clarified only by demonstrative proofs, their examination is reserved for the learned, and God excuses common men from this.

We must thus take into consideration those who have the capacity to understand rational arguments, those who are not in the habit of using them, and those who have not had the means to become educated. To the latter, God gives colorful examples (*amthāl*) and similes (*ashbāh*), leading them by these means to recognize the truth.

In summary, the Qurʾān is revealed for all men and has fundamental appeal to the human faculties that exist in everyone, to sense perceptions and the imagination, in particular. Some revealed texts are in literal agreement with rational truths. However, men capable of reflection do not need Qurʾānic revelation to know what falls into the category of demonstrative proofs. Islamic Law, which speaks to all men, can be understood by different means. Those who live at the level of sensation and imagination are touched by the beauty of the style and by the brilliance of its images: that is what has been called the inimitability of the Qurʾān (*iʿjāz al-Qurʾān*), in which believers see a miracle that proves the divine origin of the Word that descended upon the Prophet. The strength of the rhetoric becomes evident in the exhortations (*mawāʿiz*), and the dialectic is affirmed by the addition of figures and diagrams. Those who are capable of rational thought discover understandable relationships that undergird these images. It is, however, always the same truth that is apprehended through different channels. The double truth is not one of Averroes' teachings; this would be beneath the dignity of a philosopher for whom the unity of thought is an inviolable value. The only distinction that should be recognized is that of a theoretical truth and of a practical truth, a distinction that is also found in both philosophical thought and religious thought. Beyond that, if there is cause to speak of a double truth, it is only a question of two truths that mutually exclude one another; the truth of the theologians and the truth of the philosophers. It is between them that the debate takes place, and it is in criticizing the theologians through Ghazālī that Averroes will be able to defend and define Aristotelianism (which is truthful in his eyes) against the syncretism exemplified by Avicenna's system.

The Book of the Exposition of Demonstrative Methods Relative to the Teachings of Religion

The Book of the Exposition of Demonstrative Methods Relative to the Teachings of Religion is a study of what has been called the "sects" of Islam, which are really only different schools of theology. The study is far from exhaustive, and rightfully so, since these schools multiplied and differentiated themselves *ad infinitum* with nuances in which a philosopher such as Averroes had no interest. His interest was exclusively in the materialists, in the Sufis, in the Ashʿarites, and, through them, in the Muʿtazilites.

God and the world

Regarding the existence of God, some rely solely on the authority of the Qurʾān. Others make use of reason, but with questionable methods. The proof by contingency of the world goes from an effect back to its cause. Certainly, the world is contingent, because it does not exist by itself and its cause is not in itself. But this does not imply that such a being is not eternal: it should be, because its cause is. Theologians use the idea of contingency to prove the existence of a God creator conceived as an eternal first cause, while the world, in its contingency, would be temporal, produced and developed in time. They make a false idea out of contingency, an idea crafted to fit their need to convince people that the contingent world, if it is temporal, should have an intemporal cause, the eternal creator God.

Considered as starting from God, the question is simple. How could the action of an eternal being have a beginning in time? We saw in *The Short Treatise* that nowhere does the Qurʾān teach that God is alone in His eternity while nothing has yet been created, with the result that creation, which is not nothing (*ʿadam*) should, under these conditions, not be eternal. Nevertheless, the problem remains: would the world be eternal just as God is eternal, or would it be simply coeternal with God? No, it is not coeternal, since from an ontological point of view the being of the cause is superior to the being of the effect. But if there is an ontological gap between the cause and the effect, what is its nature? If a discrepancy is supposed, can it be something other than temporal? God is eternally a creator: that stems from His essence; but actual creation stems from His action. Is this action eternal? If so, it is totally subject to the divine essence. If not, then between it and essence is wedged what theologians call a *murajjih,* that is, a secondary cause which "tips the scale" in favor of the creative act. But if this *murajjih* is itself eternal, God will have created from all eternity, unless it is assumed that His efficiency took a break: this is the "*murajjih* retreat" (*tark al-murajjih*). But then, for there to be an act of creation, a rest from this rest is needed (*tark tark al-murajjih*). And the scale will need to tip in favor of these successive pauses, such that the process goes on infinitely, which proves the absurdity of the supposition that God the Creator would not create from all eternity. In more everyday terms, what would He have been doing before creating? The Qurʾān says: "God! There is no God but He, the Living, the Self-Subsisting. Neither slumber nor sleep come upon him" (Qurʾān 2:255).

Consequently, the existence of a God creator does not imply that the world is contingent, at least in the sense that it was created in time. Besides, what is time for God? We must admit that even if He is not in time, at least He knows what it is, and consequently, He knows that such and such a being will come into existence at such and such a time, or, as some Muʿtazilites say, "in its time." But this time is the time marked by the movement of the sphere, a time inside the world, not an exterior time in which the sphere and the world evolve. For Averroes as well as for Aristotle, there is nothing outside the world, neither time nor space. The time that God can know is not a time that would envelop the world since its creation. It is the very order of the successive generations that God knows since He is the Creator. It is not the time that we know *a posteriori* based on the movements of beings created in the world.

Another question raised regarding God and the world is that of atomism. In criticizing the atomism taught by the Ashʿarite School, in particular by Bāqillānī, Averroes encounters a serious—not only philosophical, but theological—problem, that of God's Almightiness and His Omniscience. There is no doubt about Islam being voluntarist: God creates what He wants and as He wants. His creation obeys no exemplary model like that of Platonic Ideas (*muthul*) a weakened reminiscence of which is found among the Muʿtazilites. To save this absolute independence of God, whose actions, completely without either motive or goal, express nothing more than pure arbitrary power, Bāqillānī turned to atomism. As in a kaleidoscope, atoms can at any time arrange themselves into different and discontinuous groupings. In this same way, the will of God can at any moment create any world it wishes and then turn it upside down a second later by a simple decree of the will. Accidents, according to this theology, do not remain naturally and by themselves on a substance in two successive moments in time. Consequently, anything can happen to anything by virtue of divine will. But how then do we explain the laws that indisputably rule the events of the world? For these theologians, they do not answer to any internal rational necessity, but depend only on the decision made by God to follow a certain order, a certain behavior (*sunna*), which is also called custom (*ʿāda*). For man, it follows that his knowledge can rely only on the observation of the regular effects of this custom, but that it cannot understand the reason why, because there is none. Besides, etymologically, intelligence (*ʿaql*) is a faculty whose role consists solely in connecting and establishing what is to come next in this manner.

Such a theology, in Averroes' opinion, downplays the wisdom and the providence of God. What is produced in each moment is an effect only because it follows what precedes it, and what precedes it is a cause only because it precedes what follows. According to Averroes, all the philosophers have recognized that pure succession could not take into account the proper nature of causality. In fact, if man, in his attempt to know, needs to seek out the cause that explains what exists by backtracking through a series of successive phenomena, he will never have a reason to stop. The cause loses all reality and is erased, to end up being only a moment in a straight line of succession that goes on infinitely. On this point Averroes is in agreement with Aristotle: infinity can be taken into consideration only in cyclical successions. Thus, the evaporation of water gives clouds, clouds give rain, and rain, water. Nevertheless, if in a straight series each term were the cause in the sense that it served as the instrument for producing the present effect of an eternal agent, this effect would in reality result from the action of this agent, and would be explained by it alone, even if the agent had used the instrument an infinity of times. Let us take the example of the living being that conceives a life after having, himself, been conceived, and so forth, *ad infinitum* in a regular succession. It might be thought that it is not this succession, as regular as it might be, that explains the constant production of the effect, the life conceived. In other words, it is not because it was first conceived that a life then conceives. Custom, that is, God's arbitrary decision to observe such a succession, does not explain anything. If God uses a life as an instrument to conceive another life, it is by giving it the ability to conceive. In the process, He creates by organizing His creation, so that human reason can discover this order and its conditions, because it has an intelligible sense and is not reduced to a simple, arbitrary (albeit constant) succession.

The Ashʿarite theologian Juwayni thought that since the world was created in a certain location in the infinity of the void, there was no reason for it to be created here rather than there; whence the necessity of a prior, free, and arbitrary decision on the part of God. But Averroes, basing himself on Aristotle's *Physics,* replied that it would be necessary to prove that an infinite void has existed from all eternity, which is not possible, since this infinite void would have to be created, and consequently situated in another infinite void enveloping it.

In fact, the Qurʾān proves God through Providence and the creation of substances that have an essential reality. If God has no end in mind when He creates, since He does not need anything, it is evident that He attributes an end to each of His creatures. This is how He makes the organic come out of the inorganic, and how He places His creation in the service of men who profit from it through their reasoning ability. This placing into service is what the Qurʾān calls *taskhīr*. The beings of the world can therefore have a purpose, although God Himself is not acting with a purpose in mind.

Contrary to the Sufis, Averroes believes that if asceticism allows detachment from the sensible and can thus favor access to rational knowledge, it cannot take the place of rational knowledge. Mystical intuition, delicious knowledge, the "taste" in which Ghazālī saw the only guarantee of certainty, are only vain pretentions, incapable of giving a firm grasp on reality. The God of the Sufis is nothing more than an illusory object, and on this point Averroes is in agreement with Avempace.

It must be remarked that in this work Averroes does not directly address the Muʿtazilites. We know that under the caliph Mutawakkil there was a marked reaction against the influence of the school: it had been the official doctrine under the preceding caliphs, and its adepts, supported by the caliph al-Maʾmūn, had unleashed a veritable inquisition, the *mihna,* directed against their established adversaries. Their works had been taken out of circulation, the result being that Averroes would scarcely have been able to know their teachings except through their adversaries' criticism in treatises of heresiography. For him, the theologians were the Ashʿarites and Ghazālī was their representative.

The Unicity of God

On the Unicity of God, the Qurʾān is especially emphatic that the world is ruled by one government. This is where the most convincing proof resides; if there were a number of gods, they would quarrel over management of the world and disorder would result. The argument is undoubtedly more rhetoric than philosophy, but it is convincing. Averroes is content to use this proof, adding depth to it with the help of Aristotle: it is in showing that the world is a perfectly coherent and organized whole that we are able to deduce that its cause, God, is singular.

The issue of attributes raised serious problems for the theologians. Is their plurality not contrary to Divine Unicity? Juwaynī had an ambiguous saying: the attributes are not God, but they are not anything other than God. The Muʿtazilites made a distinction between attributes of essence and attributes of action. The former were reduced to essence, meaning that God is knowing, powerful, and living, by His essence, not by knowledge, a power, or a life. This caused difficulties, however, since the Qurʾān speaks specifically about the knowledge that belongs to God (*ʿindahu ʿilm*, 31:34) and about a power that He possesses (*dhū'l-quwwa*, 51:58). Averroes does not dwell on this issue and dismisses his adversaries one by one, with support from the fact that the Qurʾān never even raises the question: he is content to qualify God based on His works, without stirring up the slightest problem. It is true that everyone agreed that the attributes whose names are applied to God and to man do not have exactly the same meaning: God is knowing and powerful, but not, according to the theologians, in the same way that men are. This is exact, but vague. Averroes considers this a question of pure homonyms, and he explains in what way this is so, as we saw in the case of knowledge.

God is incorporeal, contrary to what the Materialist School taught. The anthropomorphic terms used in the Qurʾān should be interpreted by keeping in mind that man needs images and that language is often itself based on images. So when believers pray, they imagine God up in the sky or beyond, although in prayer Muslims are supposed to turn toward Mecca so that they will not be tempted to divinize the heavenly bodies. It can be said that God is light, as is stated in the Qurʾān. But in everyday language the word "light" also has a figurative sense, and, since it illuminates everything, light is everywhere and nowhere. This is why the Qurʾān can say that God is "immense" (*wasīʿ*). Going back to Aristotle's conception, Averroes notes that God, being enveloped by nothing, has no location.

Divine acts

In the matter of divine acts, Averroes first looks at creation, then at justice, predestination, and the Decree, and finally at the rewards and punishments of the life to come.

The world is created, but if it contains events contingent in themselves, it could not be contingent in itself. God is of course free, but His liberty is not indifference. This does not imply that God could have chosen to create another world subject to other physical or moral laws. The idea that there is in God a will and a power distinct from one another, so that He is capable of not wanting everything that He is capable of, is a theologian's anthropomorphic idea. Averroes thinks, as have several later philosophers, that everything possible is real, that what is possible does not exceed what is real. Both are equally founded in God, and just as there is nothing outside of God, there is nothing outside of what God has made. The idea of another possible world is the product of a purely fantastic imagination. Moreover, says Averroes, the word *hudūth*, which we translate more or less successfully by "contingency," or "adventitiousness," meaning a production in the realm of the real of a pure possibility, is not of Qurʾānic origin. It is an "innovation," a *bidʿa* of theologians who wrongly separate the world of the possible from the real world; it should be condemned. Neither the Qurʾān nor the philosophical idea of God authorizes such speculation.

As we have seen, Averroes is reserved concerning the issue of the prophetic mission. In contrast to what the Eastern *falāsifa*

Fārābī, Miskaway, or Avicenna were attempting to describe, he does not ask what kind of knowledge might be specific to prophets. It is certain that he could not consider it as a kind of light radiated by God upon His Messengers. The idea of such illuminative knowledge is totally foreign to him, as it is to Aristotle. To his mind, the contents of knowledge of what is revealed to the prophets falls only in the purview of the imagination, which is normal, since it is a teaching aimed at men who live for the most part on that level. The miraculous and inimitable perfection of the language in the Qurʾān can be moving and lead to belief, but, from the evidence, it has no power of proof whatsoever. Its value is rhetorical, but not demonstrative.

Predestination raises one of the most vexing problems. There are verses for it, and verses against; likewise for the prophetic traditions (*hadīth*). Experience shows that man depends on a number of conditions that face him, but he also knows that he has the power of deliberation, using the faculties that God has given him. The theologians (with the exception of the Muʿtazilites who believed in liberty), held that since God is the creator of everything that is, man, for his part, cannot be the creator of his acts; otherwise, a single act would follow from two creative agents. But here again Averroes cautions against a univocal use of words: the word "agent" is not said solely of God and of second causes. God's being in a sense the only cause does not imply the nonexistence of second causes based on Him. God can serve as a second cause to produce an effect which, in this case, is necessary. But, because they are created by a causal power, causes can be used freely by man, endowed with the faculty of deliberating and of choosing as a function of this deliberation. Therefore, man's causality is real, but of another order than God's causality. It might be said that in giving him the faculty of deliberation, which should not remain fruitless, God places certain things at his disposal.

On the problem of justice, Averroes joins with the Ashʿarites. God is just in Himself, and everything He does is good because He does it. The concern of both the philosopher and the monotheistic believer is that of avoiding the dualism between

Good and Evil. Since Evil is real, it can only have been created by God, not as Evil as such, but in that it results from creation as an accident. Using this Aristotelian idea of accident, Averroes gives an answer to the undoubtedly unsolvable problem that is raised for both men of religion and philosophers. But it appears that this answer is scarcely satisfactory for either. Does human reason have the ability to provide a solution to this problem by demonstrative proof? There is not a great probability of this happening, and Averroes has an idea that seems to be of some importance in the matter. Man suffers from a number of evils in the world, but he knows that this situation is incomprehensible, and that philosophy will be incapable of explaining it to him. Under these circumstances, it is normal that man turns toward religon, which brings him home (*rajāʾ*) by revealing to him that God is just, that He forgives our wrongdoings, and that His Word is a guide (*hudā*) that leads to the happiness of the life beyond, just as in this life, His providence provides for creaturely needs. God is both He Who creates (*al-Khāliq*) and He Who provides (*al-Rāziq*).

Averroes admits that it is not contrary to reason that life after death is possible, even though the images presented in the Qurʾān do not prove its reality; God is content to convince men of the importance of the Law and of the interest that they have in observing it to reach the rewards promised to the faithful after death. But in a general way, when the verses related to it are dealt with appropriately, their literal sense appears both wiser and more satisfactory to Averroes than the rantings of the theologians and mystics on the subject.

In summary, in this work Averroes defends the Law by attacking interpretations that the theologians give of it. If we hold to revealed texts, it is easy to show that there is nothing that fundamentally contradicts philosophical truths, provided we understand them, if need be, according to the rules of the figurative commentary authorized by the spirit of the Arabic language. It is this detail that explains why Averroes, when he proposes an interpretation, is so attached to staying as close as possible to the letter of the texts, since this is where the language lives. Perhaps on this point he was thinking about the Zāhirite principle of understanding the word of God, in the way that Ibn Hazm of Cordoba (whom he knew well) expressed it. Thus the problem of religious truth seems, in his eyes, intimately linked to problems of the langauge and linguistic expression. This is undoubtedly the way he understood the verses where God said that He revealed the Book clearly in the Arabic language.

The Decay of Decay (*Tahāfut al-tahāfut*)

The Decay of Decay is a complex work. Its title indicates that it is aimed radically against Ghazālī's book, *The Decay of the Philosophers*. In this sense, it is a critique of theologians. But the philosophers that Ghazālī attacked were Avicenna and his followers. Averroes was opposed to Avicenna's doctrines. Consequently, in his opposition to Ghazālī's criticism of the philosophers, he was not truly defending the philosophers that Ghazālī wanted to destroy. Therefore, when an argument against Avicenna seemed just and well founded to him, he adopted it; if it appeared to be substantially just, but supported with dialectical proofs, he corrected them by replacing them with demonstrative proofs; in such a case, he criticized the method of refutation used by the theologian, but at the same time, he overthrew Avicenna's thesis, substituting for it the truth of Aristotle's thesis. After all was said and done, Averroes' aim in this book was to reestablish against Avicenna what he judged to be pure Aristotelianism, and to reclaim the value of demonstrative proof against the dialectical method of the theologians.

An exhaustive examination of this book would consequently require three comparative studies: one of Ghazālī's theology, one of Avicenna's philosophy, and one of Aristotle and Averroes. That would represent a work on almost the totality of Muslim thought. We will therefore limit our discussion to a few problems: those that pertain to God, those that pertain to the creation of the world, and those that pertain to the soul, knowledge, and the mind.

God and divine will

If the concept of God is not as clear in Greek philosophy as it is among the monotheistic thinkers, it is not absent, and the immobile Prime Mover certainly corresponds quite well to the idea of God as the first cause for the existence of the world. This Prime Mover is one of the three substances that Aristotle distinguishes: the non-sensible substance that is beyond sensible and eternal substance; that of the sky composed of the "quintessence"; and that of generable and corruptible sensible substance, composed of form and matter, which is that of the beings of the sublunar world. Since knowledge is all the more understandable, the more separated it is from matter, perfectly immaterial substance should have, or rather be, perfectly pure and understandable knowledge. In fact, at this level, as we have seen, the intellect that understands is identical to what it understands, and consequently the Prime Mover is in itself thought from thought (νοήσις νοήσεως), it is truly God. All this is Aristotelian, and Averroes needed no more than to pick it up. As a Muslim, he had no choice but to approve of the perfect transcendence of Aristotle's God, who knows what is not Him only by knowing Himself. Nevertheless, Averroes, on this point, ran up against Qurʾānic voluntarism: as we have seen, God creates what He wishes, as He wishes, and "when He decrees the existence of a thing, He says: Be! And it is (*kun fa-yakūn,* Qurʾān 2:117, 3:47, among a number of other verses)." Averroes would put an ingenious spin on this difficulty. The Prime Mover cannot set the world into motion by communicating movement to it, because it is immobile. Aristotle spoke of a kind of aspiration that attracted matter toward God by giving it a form. One might wonder if this solution is truly the result of demonstrative proof, or if it is not rather called for by the demands of the cohesiveness of the system. Whatever the case, Averroes accepted it as it was, but his idea was to illustrate it via a Qurʾānic idea, that of the divine commandment (*amr*). Granted, this idea is voluntarist, but it has the advantage of useful imagery: God creates the Universe and sets it in motion through His simple command, without needing, so to speak, to move, just like a sovereign who governs without leaving his throne (the image of the throne of God is Qurʾānic, also). Nevertheless, this interpretation is not enough for Averroes, who is led to criticize directly the idea of divine will, via an examination of what the will is. A number of the *Tahāfut*'s passages deal with the question. The theologians made a distinction between an eternal will and an adventitious will. But these two terms are pure homonyms in this usage. "The will that is in this lower world is a faculty that includes the possibility of doing one of the two opposites, and the possibility also exists to approve equally of the two objects of the will. In effect, the will is the desire that the agent has to act, and once it has acted, the desire goes away, since what was wanted has been obtained. [But the faculty of choosing still remains.] This desire and this action depend on the two opposites equally. Also, when it is said that he who wishes one of the two opposites is eternal, we downplay the definition of will, and its nature passes from possibility into existence." In fact, when we speak of an eternal will that is not suppressed by the presence of that which is wanted, which has no beginning and does not make a distinction between one moment and another as far as reaching the desired goal is concerned, "all we are doing is producing the proof of the existence of an agent endowed with a faculty that is neither voluntary nor natural, but which the Qurʾān calls 'will.'" In effect, God transcends both nature and will in His action as well as in His being.

On the other hand, he who through his will makes a free choice is a man who is lacking what he wishes. But God lacks nothing. He who chooses is a man for whom there are preferable values; but God has no need to prefer anything. Basically, the will is a passive state subject to change, since what one wants is always something that one does not have. Passivity and change do not affect God.

The theologians maintain that God's will plays an indispensable role in the creative act. If the philosophers deny that a purely adventitious event like the production of the world could be the work of an eternal agent, it is because they do not allow for the possible intervention of a will. They think that in their relationship to God, the opposites cease to exclude one another as contradictory, but unite by becoming similar. Actually, the perfect unity of an absolute intelligence demands this consequence which several philosophical systems (like that of Plotinus) had admitted. It is true that they explained the passage from unity to multiplicity through the admittedly obscure process of the degrees of emanation conceived as progressive diffusion and dispersion. But Averroes was hostile to such a system, represented in Islam by Fārābī and Avicenna. Whatever the case, according to the Muslim theologians, in order to create this world, God had to make a choice, discerning between choices that were similar only for Him, but which could not exist together in a unity outside Him. For such a distinction to be possible, a will truly needed to intervene. There is, thus, in God, a real will which manifests itself in the creative act and in all of creation.

As it exists in man, the will normally chooses from between two opposites the one that fills its desire or need. If it finds itself in the presence of two similar objects, it can choose one of the two only if there is a particularizing factor (*mukhassis*) that "tips the scale" (*yurajjihu*) in favor of one of them to the exclusion of the other (this *mukhassis* is thus called *murajjih,* as we have seen), or else it is impossible for will to be carried out and the very idea of will disappears. It is true that the Qurʾān attributes a will to God. But it is through pure homonymy, as is the case for all God's other attributes: knowledge, power, and so forth. To escape this conclusion, might it be said that the divine will is, in itself, independent of the fact that it has to choose between two opposites, or to distinguish between two likes, and that it is rather a pure potentiality of decision whatever acts might spring from it? That is undoubtedly the theologians' idea of an absolutely arbitrary divine will, but it is incomprehensible and has no relationship to the notion that we might have of a will. On the other hand, if we admit that the eternal divine will does not act and does not choose between likes, except through the action of *mukhassis,* it will follow that this action is previous to it, which is absurd. At any rate, a will that requires such a factor of determination in order to pass into action would be nothing more than a purely arbitrary faculty of decision, and the theologians' point of view would no longer be justified.

On the other hand, in contrast to what would be true for Plotinus, opposites are not reduced to likes in the case of the action of God, a creator. Actually, all the contradictory opposites come back definitively to the greatest of all oppositions: that of existence and non-existence. It might thus be thought that, when God creates, He wishes the existence of what He creates. But what is this wish that would be ordered to an end and, consequently, would not be arbitrary? To respect what they believe to be the Qurʾānic doctrine of an absolute will to decree (*mashīʾa*), the theologians point out that God, being perfect, could not propose a goal (*gharad*) for Himself. The ends are what, in action, particularize the things desired and detach them from others. But God desires nothing. To this Averroes replies that it is actually absurd to think that God has goals that perfect His essence, as the goals that we voluntarily pursue do for us. But it is not the same for goals that have as an end, not the good of him who wants, but the good of what is wanted: it is not absurd to think that God wishes them when He has His creatures pass from nonexistence into an existence that is a good. Now the "first will" never chooses from among opposites what is best (*afdal*) for the created beings. (This Arabic word is certainly synonymous with the word *aslah* used in the same sense by the Muʿtazilites, who profess divine justice by teaching that God does only good, that is, what is best for the creatures.) Averroes here clearly stands out from the Ashʿarites. Whatever the case, deep down, this will for the best, which can be described as a choice, describes no more than the excellence of the order that human reason can discover in the world and that it normally brings back to its cause, which is God. Despite the voluntarist expressions in the Qurʾān, which must be interpreted, the work of God cannot be other than wise and ordered, and it is this order that human reason is destined to recognize; it is not through the effect of arbitrary wishing that it receives the commandment to ratify.

The problem of the creation of the world

The idea of a creation certainly is of religious origin. But it is connected to the question of the beginning and the end of the world, and from this point of view it is not foreign to the speculation of philosophers about the interconnectedness of causes, about the first cause, and consequently about time, eternity, and infinity.

The philosophers affirm that the world is eternal, and the Ashʿarites oppose this teaching. The principle upon which they base their arguments is the following: if we imagine the revolutions of two moving bodies endowed with circular motion that take place between the two points of the same single time, the relationship of the partial number of revolutions of one of the two moving bodies to the partial number of revolutions of the other is the same as the relationship of the totality of the revolutions of one to the totality of revolutions of the other. "For example, if the revolution of Saturn in one year is one-thirteenth the revolutions of the sun during the same period of time, and if we imagine establishing a relationship between the totality of the revolutions of the sun and the totality of the revolutions of Saturn in a specific period of time, the relationship of the total number of revolutions of the first movement to the total number of revolutons of the second must inevitably be the same relationship as the number of partial revolutions of the first to the number of partial revolutions of the other." Now if these revolutions have been taking place for an unlimited time, and are thus infinite in number, we have in the example proposed an infinite number of revolutions that on one hand will be thirteen times greater than another infinite number of revolutions on the other hand. Since this consequence is absurd, these theologians deduce from it that there is no infinite number of revolutions of the sphere, that the time of the world is not infinite, and that it began with creation. Averroes' response is the same as Aristotle's. The argument holds if the movements of the past existed in actuality; but they are only in potentiality for a thought that is thinking of them. There can be a real relationship only between countable partial movements in actuality situated between two defined boundaries in time, not between limitless, and thus undefined, movements. Infinite thus here means undefined. Let us note, moreover, that when we wish to count circular movements, the time in which we count them is not that which numbers these movements themselves, but the time of the thought that counts them. This distinction between the inseparable time of the movement of a moving body and the time of thought is of a fundamental importance that neither Aristotle nor Averroes emphasized sufficiently, although they hint at it.

Thinking about past time raises a problem: if this time is the numbered number of past movements, can it be infinite, which would imply an infinite succession of movements? Now all movement is the effect of a preceding movement that is its cause. If we are obliged to go back indefinitely from effect to cause to realize the existence of a present movement, present motion would not exist, since, as Aristotle said, infinity cannot be crossed. If movement in the present time exists, it is that there must be an endpoint to the succession of movements in past time, or else there would be an effect without a cause, a moving body without a mover. But if this is how we interpret Aristotle's ἀνάγκη στῆναι (one must stop in going back to causes), besides the fact that this is an arbitrary decision, the result would be that motion has a beginning, that there is a first motion, a first cause of all the others, which will not therefore be preceded by any other movement and therefore by any time, in other words, that the world is created, as the theologians would have it. But is this really what Aristotle thought? Clearly not, and Averroes here makes a fundamental distinction between "being in time" and "being with time." If we think that the beginning of the world is temporal, this implies that a time previous to the world exists, like an empty receptacle that receives the existence of the world in one of its moments: in this case, the world would be "in time." Since it exists, this empty time should have been created by God, but the problem of the creation of time would be raised in the same terms and with the same difficulties as that of the creation of the world. Such a time outside of all motion would, moreover, not be time as Aristotle defines it. In addition, since it would be empty, and all its moments equivalent, how would the moment of creation be determined? This is a question that we will encounter again in the subject of the creative action of God. Consequently, saying that the world is in time, created in time, does not absolutely solve the problems raised. In reality, the world is with time; that is, where the world is, there is time, and where there is time, the world is. A time that exceeds the existence of the world is the pure product of the imagination. The imagination cannot help but pretend that time exists beyond all defined time. The ἀνάγκη στῆναι means therefore that an end must be put to the fictions of the imagination, and that we must rely on demonstrative proof that there is a first and eternal motivating principle. It is Aristotle's First Mover who, by attraction, moves the spheres in their eternal revolutions, without needing to enter into time since its action, not being a movement, is atemporal.

The question of the essence of the creative action specifically remains. Averroes needs to refute one objection, according to which there was a gap between God's essence and His action. The theologians admitted the idea, thinking they could deny the eternity of the creative action of a creator God, which would have entailed the eternity of the world they reject. But such a gap supposes the introduction of time into eternity. If God remained in His eternal existence without creating, then created, what does this gap mean, what justifies and explains it, and of what does it consist? This is one of many unsolvable questions.

Averroes' reply is that the gap between the essence of the agent and His action has meaning only for a being that has a future in time. When we think the past and the beings that exist in it, and we think the eternal God, we imagine that during all this past time the Creator never ceased to be. Moreover, we can only imagine what is eternal as what has never ceased to be and will not cease to be (*lam yazal wa lā yazāl*). But this temporal mental representation of the eternal is relative to us. Consequently, when we bring everything that is in the past back to a being who has never ceased to be during all the elapsed time, that does not mean that this being has himself been present in all the past, at least if we make an abstraction of the workings of the imagination. But then: "It is not true to say that what is past and connected to the being that has not ceased to be—that is, that has not become detached from it—has entered into existence, since saying that it *entered* is the opposite of saying that it is connected to eternal existence." Consequently, if we look at the world as attached to the eternal God as well as to its cause, it is not true that it entered into existence, that is, that it had a beginning in time. In other words, it is inconceivable that there is in God a gap between His being and His action, for that would suppose that the expression "He has not ceased to be" means that His existence is a constant temporal duration, which is false. "Thus, there is no difference here between action and existence, that is, he who admits the possibility of the existence of a being that has not ceased to be in the past should accept that there are, there, acts which have not ceased to be earlier in the past, and this does not imply that the acts of this being come into existence, just as it is not implied in the continuity of its essence (*istimrār dhātihi*) that it, itself, came into existence."

But what does the anteriority of the creator God mean in relation to the world?

This question was examined by Ghazālī in the text that deals with what we looked at above, and which deserves to be cited here: "The philosophers claim that he who says that the world is posterior to God and God is anterior to it means by that that God is anterior by essence, and not by time, like the anteriority of 1 to 2, which is what it is by nature [. . .], or like the anteriority of the cause in respect to the effect, like that of movement of a person in respect to the movement of his shadow, or the movement of the hand with respect to the movement of the ring, or of the hand in water with respect to the movement of the water. In effect, the movements are simultaneous, although some are causes and the others are effects [. . .]. If that is what is meant by the anteriority of the creator God with respect to the world, it follows that the two are simultaneous; it is of little importance that the two be adventitious, or eternal. It is actually impossible that one of them be adventitious and the other eternal. Or else, he means that the Creator is anterior to the world and to time, not by essence, but according to time; before the existence of the world and of time, there would have been a time in which the world was nonexistent, since nonexistence precedes existence, and God precedes according to an extended duration with an endpoint on one side, but not on the other. Consequently, before time there would have been a limitless time, and that is contradictory. This is why the teaching of the adventitiousness of the world is impossible. And if it is necessary for time to be eternal, since it is the expression of the quantity of movement, it would be necessary for movement to be eternal; and if movement is eternal, it would be necessary for the moving body to be eternal, since it lasts for the duration of the movement."

This last proof of the eternity of the world, which Ghazālī falsely attributes to the philosophers, is lacking in worth. As we see, it is founded on two arguments. The first is this: if we do not allow that God is temporally anterior to the world, He is anterior as a cause is by its essence, and the example of a man and his shadow is offered; the man's movement is anterior to the shadow's, because he is essentially its cause, yet the two movements are nevertheless simultaneous. Let us apply this example to God and the world. Does it explain what the philosophers want to demonstrate, that is, that the world is eternal, just as God is, because their existences are simultaneous, like a cause and its effect, the movement of a man and the movement of his shadow? But as soon as one says "simultaneity," one also says "temporality." The contemporaneous causes of their effects exist only in time, just like a man and his shadow. Consequently, saying that the creative action of God and the created world exist simultaneously does not mean that the world is eternal like God, but, on the contrary, that God and His creative action are in time and that eternity is nothing other than a time "that has not ceased and will never cease," like a person who thinks about his imagination, incapable of placing a beginning point on it in the past or an endpoint in the future.

The second argument falsely attributed to the philosophers is more subtle. It consists in turning over the theologians' idea that God creates in a moment of time that is created empty as a receptacle of creation. Actually, there is no time without movement, and if there had been a time that preceded the act of creation, it would have been necessary, according to Aristotle, for it to be the numbered number of the movement of an already existent moving body. This is true, but does it prove that the world is eternal? No, since showing that if we allow hypothetically, with the theologians, that there is a time previous to the act of creation, we are led to a positive conclusion concerning the eternity of the world. This does not prove that the world is eternal, since the argument is based entirely on the criticism of the adversary's thesis, allowed hypothetically only with a view toward destroying it. It is nothing more than a simple *ad hominem* argument aimed at establishing that in wishing to prove creation, the theologians use reasons that, on the contrary, should make them recognize that the world is eternal. That is not a true demonstrative proof of the eternity of the world, and Ghazālī was mistaken in attributing it to the philosophers.

In another area, Ghazālī stressed the difficulties that arise from verbal expressions. In French and English, verb conjugations have tenses; in Arabic verb conjugations have only two aspects: the accomplished and the incomplete, depending on whether the action is considered finished or still in progress. Under the influence of the Greeks, Arabian grammarians believed that, in contrast to nouns, verbs express time, so that they more or less made the accomplished correspond to the past tense and the incomplete to the future tense, the present being rendered either by an accomplished, or by a present participle. Ghazālī asks what meaning to give to *kānaʾllāhu,* since the verb *kāna* is a perfective. Is it "God was," or "God is"? Ghazālī attempts to eliminate ideas of time, concentrating his thought solely on the idea of existence, with no temporal specificity. If we say: *kānaʾllāhu wa lā ʿālam, thumma kāna wa kāna maʿahuʾl-ʿālam* (God is [or was], and not the world, since God is [or was], and with Him is [or was] the world), this verbal expression signifies purely and simply on the one hand the existence of the Creator's essence and the non-existence of the world's essence, and on the other, the existence of two essences. Thus, in this sense, the existence of God can be conceived of without the existence of the world, which implies that the world is not eternal, as God is.

Averroes is quite severe when it comes to this argument, which he calls false and fraudulent (*khabīth*). His criticism is easily understood when we note that Ghazālī, without saying a word about it, surreptitiously uses the word *thumma* (then), and thus reintroduces time without appearing to. Ghazālī can be considered correct by the principle that later philosophers explained, but which was already germinal in Avicenna, that what is conceived separately exists separately. But this is not Averroes' point of view, and to counter Ghazālī's argument he writes: "There is demonstrable proof that these are two different kinds of existence: one, which is of the nature of movement that is not separate from time, and the other, which is not of the nature of movement and which is eternal [. . .] The first is an existent being, knowable by the senses and by the mind; the second has demonstrable proof of its existence, for whoever recognizes that all moving bodies have a mover, that everything that is made has a maker and that the causes that move one another are not without end, but end at a first, absolutely immobile cause. There is also demonstrable proof that what is not in the nature of movement is the cause of the existence of that which is in the nature of movement. And finally, there is demonstrable proof that the being that is in the nature of movement is inseparable from time, and the being that is not in the nature of movement is absolutely not touched by time. Since such is the case, the anteriority of existence that does not touch time is neither temporal anteriority nor the anteriority of cause and effect, like that of the man relative to his shadow, both of which are of the nature of moving existence. This is why everyone is mistaken who compares the anteriority of the immobile being relative to the moving being to the anteriority of two moving beings relative to one another." Averroes concludes that the anteriority of the creator God over the created world "is the anteriority of that which does not change and is not in time relative to the changing being that is in time. This is a case of antecedence of a different sort. And if such is the case, it is not true to say either that the world and God are together, or that one is anterior to the other."

The human soul, intellect, and the teaching on the mind

We have seen that Averroes supports the unity of the human soul. All of its activities are connected, from those of the nutritive life to those of the intellectual life, one setting the stage for the other. Everything in the human soul is human, even what man seems to have in common with other living beings, the animals and plants. On the other hand, Averroes never ceases to rail against the idea of emanation expressed in the writings of the Eastern philosophers Fārābī and Avicenna, and against the related teaching of the existence of a cosmic intellect, that of the sphere of the moon, which is the last in the procession of intellects emanating from the One, whose function would be to give intelligible forms to the human intellect: the *dator formarum*, likened to the Angel Gabriel of Revelation and to Aristotle's "active intellect." All these teachings are nothing more than figments of the imagination. For Averroes, the active intellect is not outside the soul, and this point is of the greatest importance.

It should first be remarked that the soul apprehends the existence of many things without apprehending their definition; otherwise, if we apprehended the definition of the soul with its existence, we would know with certain knowledge, through its existence, that it is or is not in the body. It is correct to say that we feel the soul to be in the body, as Ghazālī says, even though we do not know in which of the body's organs it is located. The Ancients argued greatly over the question of "locations," which was dealt with by the great translator from Greek to Arabic, Qusṭā Ibn Lūqā, in his *Book of Characters*. Whatever the case, knowing in such a way that the soul is in the body is not knowing with certainty that the body enters into its constitution. It is not self-evident. Ancients and Moderns were in disagreement on this point, "for if the body is for the soul like an instrument, the soul is not constituted by it, and if the body is for the soul the receptacle of that which comes to it, the soul has existence only through the body." Hence the alternative: either the body is the instrument of the soul and does not play a role in its constitution, or it is the place where the states of the soul are produced, and the soul does not exist without it. It is clear that the soul can serve the body, and in this sense we speak of the organs of the body, but it is equally clear that everything that happens to the soul does not always take place in the body. In fact, the soul is more than the simple user of the body; to be an instrument of the soul, the body must be not only constituted as a body endowed with organs, but also as capable of serving as an instrument for a soul. For Averroes, if the soul is thus necessarily appropriate for its body, it is because it gives it the appropriate form, and thus the body depends on it, and not the inverse. This is why it cannot happen that any which soul animates any which body, although any worker can make use of any tool of his trade that he finds already made and outside himself. It is from this point of view that Averroes, like all the *falāsifa*, it might be added, rejects metempsychosis. It is thus the human soul that makes a body a human body, organized just as it ought to be. And it is in this sense that Aristotle's definition should be understood, that the soul is the first entelechy of a body endowed with organs. According to its etymology, entelechy is actually an ontological perfection. It is a form. Now it is true that Aristotle taught that neither form nor matter exists separately outside of their compound. The existence of the soul would then not be separable from the existence of the body. Their union, in potentiality, would be the effect of the action of a cause in actuality: this is how man, existing in actuality, engenders man. But does this go back to infinity? If we consider, not the succession of men from father to son, but the human essence in each man in existence, there is room to think that it is his specific human form that makes of his body a specific human body. Thus, as we have seen, the definition of the soul by Aristotle is not satisfactory in Averroes' eyes, if it is considered as common to all souls, that is, abstracted, in the present case, from the existential reality of human souls. But if it is the soul that causes the body to be organized into a human body, if it is the soul that is the source of the activity of all its organs, it follows that it is dependent neither on the body's essence nor on its existence.

Under these conditions, when the body dies, it does not follow that the soul dies. But this raises a problem. On the one hand, Ghazālī, as a theologian, holds that the soul is not separate from the body, and that man is one, body and soul. It will thus follow that if the soul is immortal, the body must resuscitate. But in affirming this religious belief, Ghazālī stood in opposition to Avicenna, according to whom the multiplicity of souls is due to the multiplicity of bodies; but if the soul is one from all points of view in the totality of individuals, what results, says Averroes, is all the absurdities that we have already pointed out. Moreover, since individual souls are connected to the multiplicity of bodies, they should disappear as such with the disappearance of these bodies. All that will remain will be the universal soul. But this is not what Averroes taught. "The philosophers can say that this consequence does not impose itself. When two things have a relationship of attachment (ʿalāqa) or love (muhabba) between them, like the relationship between the lover and the beloved, or between iron and a magnet, it will not necessarily follow that when one of the two disappears, so does the other."

Nevertheless, Averroes recognized that the philosophers need to demonstrate in what way souls are individuated and multiplied numerically when, according to them, souls are separate from matter: this is the serious problem of individuation. But how has it been raised? If there is an essence of man that makes all men be men, what makes Socrates a man, except if the human form molds a material body that is his? Such is the teaching of individuation by matter. Taken to the extreme, this teaching would make what is specifically Socrates a pure effect of matter, which is not receivable. So Socrates' body must not be pure matter receiving a form, but it must be informed by what makes it into Socrates' body. "From there, Plato proved that the soul is separate from the body because the soul gives it proportion and form, which would not be the case if the body were a condition of its existence." On this point, we have just seen that Averroes thinks likewise, since he recognizes that material forces are incapable, in their working, of giving the required forms through the order of the world. "We know that the soul is something more than natural warmth, which is not apt for performing ordered and intelligible acts, just as we know that the warmth that is in seeds does not have sufficient capacity for giving form and proportion." But for Averroes, it is the soul of each man that performs this formative function, while for the Platonics there are souls in all animal beings, vegetable or mineral, which, to be engendered and to subsist, need potentialities that govern them and that are intermediary souls, between celestial souls and the souls here below in sensible bodies. We can here recognize the cosmological point of view of the Neoplatonic thinkers that are, for Averroes, the *falāsifa* of Islam against whom his pure Aristotelianism stood in opposition.

In closing, we shall examine the question of the resurrection of the body. Ghazālī accused the philosophers of denying it. Averroes begins by remarking that the first to speak of the resurrection of the body were the prophets of Israel who came after Moses. "It is clear in the Psalms and in a number of texts in the Bible. It is likewise affirmed in the Gospels and the sayings of Jesus that are reported. It is also the doctrine of the Sabeans, whose Laws, according to Ibn Hazm, are the oldest of all." The philosophers, coming after the prophets, understood that religious laws are necessary for the existence of practical and theoretical virtues that cannot be acquired except through moral virtues, which "are only possible through the knowledge of God, through adoration of Him, through set manners of worship, and through the laws of each religion: sacrifice, prayer, invocation." There is no doubt that, for Averroes, the utility of religious laws was above all that of values that are of a political order (*madaniyya*). But life in community is a reality, and that which is capable of organizing it and governing it participates in its reality. The intellect has principles in this respect. But it is difficult to have certain knowledge of them, and especially to apply them; the religions are here of inestimable assistance "especially in that which is common to all the Laws, even though they may differ from one another to a greater or lesser extent." The philosophers saw that these Laws should not be exposed in the form of affirmative or negative teachings in relation to their own general principles; but that there is room to consider "that all these Laws are in agreement in affirming a final existence after death, even though they differ as to the nature that can be attributed to this existence [. . .]. The philosophers agree, likewise, about the actions that lead to happiness in the life hereafter, although they differ in their determination. In a general sense, since these Laws are oriented toward wisdom through a channel common to everyone, wisdom is obligatory in their opinion, whereas philosophy is only oriented toward the definition that makes happiness known *to certain men endowed with understanding*" [I have chosen the alternate expression: *li-ba'd al-nās al-'uqalā'*]. But men only attain this happiness in association with one another, and they all receive a general teaching in their religious communities in view of this end. Also, when a man has reached his maturity, he should not disregard the beliefs with which he was brought up, and if he is a philosopher, he should use *ta'wīl* in the best fashion, as we have seen. "If he shows doubt about the principles of the Law with which he was educated, or if he holds to an allegorical commentary [which Averroes distinguishes from true *ta'wīl*], know that he stands in opposition to the prophets, that he is straying from their paths and that he is, of all men, the most worthy of being called *kāfir*, which forces the religion in which he was raised to punish him for infidelity." We thus see that religious beliefs should be respected for political and social reasons. Similarly, since they assure the existence and order of communities, which are unquestionably realities, they reflect a practical truth whose expression is in accord with moral and philosophical truths, either to the letter or through an appropriate *ta'wīl*. The same is true for practical truth as for speculative truth, and the revealed law that leads to happiness is true in this sense.

After these considerations comes a remarkable passage where a concept of tolerance that, in a way, is a perfect example of

Muslim thinking can be seen. "This being the case, man should choose the best religious confession (*milla*) of his time, even though in his eyes all of them are true. He should believe that the best is abrogated by the one that is better than it [. . .]. This is why the sages who taught in Alexandria became Muslims when the Law of Islam reached them. This is why the sages who were in Rome became Christians when the Law of Jesus came to them. No one doubts that there were sages among the Children of Israel, and that is manifest in the books that they attribute to Solomon. Wisdom has never ceased to exist among inspired men, and this is why there is nothing more true than the judgment that all prophets are sages, even though every sage is not a prophet; the sages are learned men who are said to be the inheritors of the prophets."

A number of interesting Qurʾānic ideas show up in this text: the idea of the "niche of prophecy," where the light that guides men is kept (cf. Sura 24:35) and which, according to the commentators, instructs the prophets, the masters of philosophy, according to a quite ancient belief about Moses, transmitted primarily by Philo of Alexandria; the idea that God revealed His Law to all generations of men since the time of Adam; the idea that Laws succeed one another in history, that the Law of Jesus superceded that of Moses, just as that of Muhmammad abrogates the laws of Jesus and Moses. The teaching of abrogation (*naskh*) is fundamental in Islam; it plays a great role in the exegesis of the jurists in distinguishing, among Qurʾānic verses, those that announce or put an end to rules that are legal prescriptions; and it is not surprising that Averroes, a specialist in legal principles (*uṣūl al-fiqh*) makes space for it. Finally, this passage is driven by the consideration that the Qurʾān gives to the "People of the Book" (*Ahl al-Kitāb*), Jews and Christians, who received a revelation and who, if they wish to remain attached to their own law, should not be treated as infidels. Nevertheless, it does not speak explicitly about the situation of the *dhimmi,* the People of the Book admitted as "protégés" of the Muslim community. However, that was not his purpose here.

Averroes concluded that "if we grant that it is possible to legislate in these matters by the intellect alone, we are forced to admit the greatest value of laws drawn from both intellect and Revelation at the same time." We should fully understand that the testimony of the Book adds nothing to the certitude of demonstrative proof, but instead of concerning only the learned, it touches all men, including the learned who know how to practice *taʾwīl* appropriately. From this point of view, men on the whole need to follow the teaching of the prophets by imitation (*taqlīd*), just as the common faithful follow the teaching of the doctors. That being said, Averroes shows the superiority of Islamic Law. For example, the institution of Muslim prayer makes it more perfect than it is in other religions, by virtue of the conditions of number, of time, and of the nature of the invocations that are prescribed.

It is also on the matter of the life hereafter, of the return to God (*maʿād*), that Islam stands out. What it says in this regard "is what is most inciteful of virtuous actions." This is why prophetic teaching, in order to speak of the life hereafter, uses examples that are rich in images, "which is more worthwhile than taking examples made from spiritual illustrations." Like many of his fellow Muslims, Averroes believed that if the Jews placed too much emphasis on the material side of the Law, the Christians erred in seeing only the spiritual side: Islam holds to the happy medium. But the Prophet said that in Paradise there are things which no eye has seen, which no ear has heard, and about which no human being has spoken. One of the oldest and most authoritative interpreters of the Qurʾān, Ibn ʿAbbās, "said that, in the Life Hereafter, all that remains in this world are names." Averroes says that, with these words, he is showing "that this existence is a new production, superior to the one here below, a better way of being (*tūr*)." But we should not think that we can apprehend the transformation (*intiqāl*) of one of these modes of being into another in the same way that we apprehend the transformation of fixed forms in matter (*al-suwar al-jamādiyya*) into the forms of intelligible essences. The latter passage takes place in this world, and can be the object of experience or of demonstration, which is something very different from a passage from this life to the Life Hereafter. But it suffices that the life hereafter be possible, given what was said of the human soul, and that its reality be required by men's happiness.

What Ghazālī says in his opposition to Avicenna's philosophy is excellent. "Yes, the soul is immortal, as rational and religious proofs show. But what returns at the *maʿād* are beings that resemble (*amthāl*) the bodies that were here below, and not these bodies themselves, because what has been annihilated does not come back in its individuality." In regard to the resurrection of the body, moreover, the Qurʾān always speaks of a second creation.

In conclusion, since the human soul is one, the different intellects that have been distinguished by Aristotle's commentators are, according to Averroes, no more than relative aspects of the different activities of the soul. On this point, Averroes does not follow Aristotle to the letter where the Stagirite says that the "active mind" that produces all the objects of mind "is separate, impassible, and without mixture" (*De Anima* III, 430a15). But these characteristics could very well be the very ones that Averroes attributes to the human intellect considered as an entelechy in the sense that he gives to this word, as we have seen. What is sure is that the texts of the *Treatise on the Soul* are far from clear, which proves, moreover, the diversity of the commentaries that were done on it by the Greeks, and which Averroes knew, cited, explained, and critiqued. Thus, when Aristotle says that "the intellect is the form of forms," while the context suggests that he is referring to the human intellect and that, as the form of forms, it could be neither material nor passive, can it not be thought that such expressions justify Averroes' interpretation, which was also that of Saint Thomas?

Moreover, Aristotle defined the material intellect as a part of the soul in the potentiality of knowing the objects of intellect. For Averroes, it is the soul itself as the incorporeal and impassive receptacle that receives them but without suffering as a result of any action that they take on it, or from the action of an exterior intellect that might give them to it, as Fārābī would have had it. Definitively, the material intellect and the active intellect are just two aspects of the soul. A text discovered by the Egyptian

Mahmoud Kassem (Mss. 1009, Fol. 144, V. C. 2) sums this question up perfectly: "There are in our soul two kinds of action: one, which is that of making the objects of intellect, the other, which is that of receiving them. Insofar as it makes the objects of intellect it is called active [intellect], and in so far as it receives them, it is called passive, but it is the single same entity."*

---

*M. Kassem. *Théorie de la connaissance d'après Averroès et son interprétation chez Thomas d'Aquin.* Algiers: Société Nationale d'Édition et de Diffusion, 1978/79, p. 212.

CONCLUSION

A Personal Muslim Thinker

Our plan has been to show the unity between Averroes' life and his work. His activities as a jurist, as a physician, and as a commentator on Aristotle, form a perfectly coherent whole with his personal life as well as his social life, with his thought as well as his religious beliefs. Without a false note, he was able to bring harmony to his education as a jurist in his family background, and to his medical and philosophical education among his contacts with the famous men of the time. There is absolutely no reason to judge the fact that he was, in the depths of his being, what we call a free thinker, and that he must have had to mask carefully his most intimate convictions in order to escape the threats of a politically powerful religious orthodoxy. His ideas, and his attacks against the theologians especially, undoubtedly earned him a number of enemies. It would have been normal. But the hostility of several doctrinarians did not disturb him to the point that it got him to bend. Moreover, it would be historically inaccurate to believe that he was persecuted: in fact, he enjoyed the favor of caliphs, except for a short time toward the end of his life when he fell into disgrace, even though this was the unfortunate consequence of a political situation in which he was not personally implicated.

His philosophical thinking in itself is not original, since it is entirely tributary to Aristotle's system. But Averroes' goal was to reestablish a pure Aristotelianism, free of any syncretism that marred, particularly, the Neoplatonism of the eastern *falāsifa*. In so doing, he was led to deepen a certain number of fundamental philosophical ideas concerning the human soul, knowledge, space, time and eternity, what is necessary, what is possible, and what is real. On these different questions, he had points of view that can be compared to those of much more recent thinkers, like Spinoza (regarding the real and the possible), and especially Kant (on the one hand regarding the idea that space and time are linked to the imagination that takes them with it constantly and everywhere in all knowledge, and on the other regarding the concept of religion from a philosophical and political point of view).

Averroes had no followers in the Muslim world. But we do know that he had considerable influence on the Jews: a number of his works were translated into Hebrew, some of which were even known only through Hebrew translations. Finally, the important role he played in the history of Medieval Latin thought, along with the Jewish Maimonides, is well known. Saint Thomas Aquinas used his commentaries. But the Latin Averroists must be cited above all: Siger de Brabant, John of Jandun, and the Paduan School made famous by Renan.

It is certain that in the history of Muslim thought Averroes deserved a fate different than that which awaited him. Might he still have a role to play in the treatment of the cultural and political problems that are today shaking up the Muslim world? Certainly, the contents of his teachings carry the mark of Medieval systems. But it seems unquestionable that his openness of mind, his rigorous method, the perspecuity of his analyses, not to mention his innovations, several of which have meaning for us or put us onto the path of new research, and finally, and perhaps especially, the frank and direct manner in which he approached difficulties and attempted to solve them while avoiding the slightest fraudulent sophism (*khabīth*), are examples that deserve to be pondered and which can still be profitably utilized today in the teaching of philosophy and in planning for the education of young thinkers for our time.

It seems indubitable that Averroes was conscious of creating a philosophical work sheltered from all the forms of illuminism of which the Eastern thinkers could be accused. We know that

Avicenna's personal thought, in particular, has been able to be interpreted in an esoteric sense by Henry Corbin, in his explanation of the term "Oriental philosophy" (*al-hikmat al-mashriqiyya*) and in his exposé of the triology of the *Récits mystiques* (Hayy ibn Yaqzān, "The Living Son of the Awakened One," the story of the Bird, and Salāmān and Absāl), where there is both an invitation to a voyage, and an actual voyage toward the Orient of Lights. The idea of emanation (*fayd*) inherited from Neoplatonism that had inspired the Greek gnostics rules the cosmological structure of Fārābī's system and shows up again in the Ismaili gnosticism of the Brothers of Purity, which was well received in Spain. The comparison of the active intellect to an angel outside the human soul comes out of this view of the hierarchical architecture of the universe. Nothing is more foreign to Averroes' thinking: he was resolutely rationalist and based his thought on data from the sensory world. Metaphysics is not a primordial knowledge at the origin of all sciences; it is what comes *after* the sciences, whose principles—which each science puts to work as a transitory hypothesis—it justifies. It is like the keystone that finishes off the building and holds it together, but which could never be at the base of the construction. In this, Averroes is faithful to what Aristotle taught in the *Posterior Analytics* (I, 72b25 ff.): "It is impossible for the same things to be both anterior and posterior at the same time, unless one says [. . .] that some are anterior and clearer for us, and the others anterior and clearer absolutely. But in this case [. . .], knowing would, in reality, be of two kinds. Would it not be better to think that the form of demonstration whose point of departure is truths better known to us is not demonstration properly speaking?" Thus it is only secondarily that metaphysics, by establishing demonstrations properly speaking, rises up to truths that are anterior in themselves, but not for us.

On the other hand, there is no reason to think that Averroes did not take his duties as cadi seriously, like a good Muslim. Likewise, it would be contrary to Averroes' teaching of the total unity of man, body and soul, a sensible being and a rational being, to believe that he might have led a double life split by an impenetrable screen: that of philosopher and that of judge. We have seen that he accorded full importance to the idea that Qurʾānic revelation is the revelation of a law, and that he had to apply it in his function as Grand Cadi. The entire Qurʾān is, in his eyes, composed of verses the purpose of which is to convince the common man of the need to obey God's commandments, the commandments of a God who presents Himself as a creature, who sees to all the needs of His creatures, who knows the weakness of men, but who specifically helps them and guides them through His Law, who threatens them with the punishments of hell if they rebel, and who, in order to lead them to obedience, promises rewards via the attractions of the joys of Paradise. The aim of this whole aspect of the Qurʾān is to touch men who are sensitive only to the pleasures and pains of their bodies. But such verses should not leave indifferent those sages who should know that a revelation of this kind is indispensable for such men, and who have the duty, in the Muslim community, of not neglecting them. And is the duty of the cadi not precisely that of upholding respect for the Law for the greater good of the Prophet's *umma* and each of its members?

There is perhaps another way of looking at Revelation, even, and especially, when one is a philosopher who wonders about the conduct of human life. In addition to the speculative life, there is also private life. The practical intellect can undoubtedly define good and evil, what is useful and what is harmful, the better and the preferable as opposed to the worse and the abhorrent, but it is difficult, even impossible, for it to set the basis for a moral obligation that is imposed on all. As an individual, man can have the sense of his duty; but from where does he draw it, and how could he extend it to others? Is it the result of a social constraint to which everyone is subject? Perhaps, but on this point, Averroes had the living example of all Muslims, of the power that belonging to the Prophet's community exercised on each of the faithful; this force was based on faith in the truth of the verses that teach the value of this, the best of all communities, in the eyes of God. Qurʾānic verses abound on this subject. For example 2:143: "We have made of you a community of the happy medium so that you might be witnesses among men"; or 3:110: "You are the best of the communities created for you; you command what is good and you forbid what is evil" (cf. 3:104). It might be remarked that these verses are speaking about the Muslim community as the respository of a moral norm contained in the Law. Thus the obligation comes from God and thereafter is imposed on all men. In reserving a central space for Qurʾānic revelation, therefore, Averroes did not err, either as a Muslim cadi or as a philosopher in search of a foundation for duty.

Nevertheless, can Averroes' God satisfy all believers? The speculative theologians spoke about faith and works, and asked themselves if works are or are not indispensible for true faith. For many, the affirmation of the unicity of God (*tawhīd*) and submission (*islām*) to His will and His decree seems to be what is essential. The mystics, however, move the interior life in its relationship to God into the foreground. As we have seen, Averroes was not a mystic. It seems that, for him, proclamation of *tawhīd* and submission were implied by the practice of good works. It is thus normal to think that to his mind what counted in defining a Muslim was good works, which is not surprising for a jurist and a cadi.

Whatever the case, Averroes' conception of God is more philosophical than religious. This is explained by the fact that he wrote about it through his criticism of Avicenna's "theology" and ontology, founded on the idea of God as a necessary being. On this point, moreover, he is quite close to the Qurʾān, which reveals the existence and unicity of God along with the means of convincing oneself by observing the wonders of the created world, without saying anything of His essence. The multiplicity of attributes had raised a serious problem for theologians who feared that it would destroy a sense of God's unity. Averroes thinks that the divine essence, which is not revealed to us, is translated for us by the different attributes, depending on the point of view from which we consider God. Nevertheless, the attributes, although relative to human thought, are not reduced to that: they have a foundation in the inscrutable richness of the essence. The attributes express the perfection of the divine essence, but they add nothing to it. These observations do touch on questions stirred up by speculative Muslim theology, *kalām*.

But they have only a distant relationship to the religious life of the simple believer, to whom Averroes' ideas were somewhat disappointing.

But for a religious soul, discussions about the attributes were undoubtedly of little importance: they applied to the general idea of attribute, not to their nature itself. What does the Qurʾān say about this? That God pardons, that He turns toward those who come back to Him, that He loves those who abandon themselves to Him and undergo trials with constancy, that He remembers those who keep Him in their memories, that He appreciates those who abide with Him. In short, it is said in the Qurʾān that God is He who speaks, He to whom one speaks, He about whom one speaks; in other words, He is a person. Only the Muslim mystics were interested in this aspect of Qurʾānic revelation. But it should be recognized that they held a marginal position in Islam. If some theologians were Sufis, if there is a mystical theology (clearly expressed in Qushayrī's *Risāla*), *kalām* on the whole is speculative thought. Thus, it was in his own speculation that Averroes rose up against this method, which he accused of being purely dialectic. Under the circumstances, what was there for him to do after eliminating esoteric commentary, mysticism, and speculative theology from his Islam? All that was left to do was what he did: he affirmed and showed the value of the Muslim law and explained how verses revealed for the use of the common man, and not the learned as such, could agree with philosophical truths, founded on demonstrative reasons.

There is another point that causes difficulty in Averroes' religious thinking, and that regards life after death. On a number of occasions the Qurʾān distinguishes between this life (*hayāt al-duniā*) and the Life Hereafter (*al-ākhira*). The common believer is certainly touched by the promises of Paradise and the threats of Hell, and after his death he hopes to enjoy the delights of the Garden of Eden. However, it is evident that such beliefs cannot be supported by demonstrable proofs. At the most, one can attempt to show that they are possible, or at least not impossible, as far as reason is concerned. Does Averroes go that far? It appears so, as we shall see.

Avicenna thought he could assure the survival of the soul by his idea of the intellect separated from matter, and thus independent of the perishable body. But what then becomes of the teaching of the resurrection of the body? Ghazālī had clearly pointed out the insufficiency of such a teaching in the eyes of faith. Averroes, for his part, recognized that the activity of the human intellect does not diminish with the advancing age of the body, and he considered, along with Aristotle, that since it knows the universal, it works without corporal organs. Consequently, it is immortal. But given that it is an object foreign to all that is individual, its immortality could not be that of an individual person. Averroes noted that this argument only took into account the intellect in the general notion that we can have of it, and that it is true as far as what concerns it from this point of view. But what about the human intellect? Since, according to him, the human soul is perfectly one, from the nutritive faculty to the intellective faculty, the case of the human intellect could not be separated from the case of the other potentialities of the soul. So vision can weaken, because the organ of the eye has weakened with age or accidentally, but not because the faculty of vision has been affected and has degenerated. This point stands out when Aristotle talks about an old man who would see just as he had in his youth if someone gave him a young man's eyes. In short, the accidents that affect the bodily organs in sleep, as well as physical shortcomings, illnesses, and old age, only disturb the exercise of the faculties and the exterior manifestation of their acts; but nothing proves that the faculties themselves, as powers of the soul, are affected. Such a point of view leads to the thought that in the unity of the soul, the faculties, even if they act through the body's organs, are nevertheless not corporal realities, but they themselves continue to be of a purely psychic nature. In the unity of the soul, the hierarchy of faculties forms a whole that is commanded by the intellect, the final entelechy to which the totality of the human soul is subordinate.

All these considerations only develop one of Aristotle's statements, but they do not constitute an apodictic demonstration.

At the most, they open the way to a likelihood and a possibility. The convincing force of rational argument applies only to the intellect taken by itself, that is, considered as separable and separate. But that is an abstraction, relative to the indivisible reality that man is. Given this, Averroes admits that the question of the soul taken as a whole is obscure to the highest point (*jāmid jiddan*). It is the domain of the "unshakable" men of learning to be able to venture into this darkness without danger of losing courage. Is he here talking about philosophers armed with a rational method of investigation? No, for then their method should dissipate the darkness, and the question would become clearer. These learned individuals are simply presented in contrast to the masses (*jumhur*) to whom imaged Revelation is addressed. In what way are they unshakable (*rāsikhūn*)? In order to understand this, let us not forget that, according to Averroes, there are problems that arise ineluctably, but which the philosopher cannot solve, even though he does know why their solutions elude philosophical research. For the most part, these are the problems of origins and final ends. We see this in the problem of the creation of the world, and even in that of the immortality of the soul. Human reason is incapable of encompassing such problems, and it knows so, because in order to do so it would have to leave time and its representation, which is impossible, since it cannot detach itself from the imagination, which is inextricably linked to spatio-temporal intuition. Man should thus not delve into these real yet also unsolvable questions unless he has a solid, unshakable faith. But the common man would risk despair unless God sent him an imaged answer. It comes from the analogy to sleep: "God gathers souls at the moment of death, as well as those that do not die during their sleep" (39:42). This analogical argument, said Averroes, "is an indication (*dalīl*) that fits for everyone; it serves to make the masses believe in the truth; it warns the learned about the road to follow for information about the survival of the soul." It is thus a question of information, not of demonstration.

The clearest result is that the death of the body does not imply the death of the soul taken in its unity and its totality. The use of bodily organs by some of these faculties does not cut them off from the whole by setting the intellect aside and reserving immortality for it alone. This is all the philosopher can say, but in so saying, he happens to agree with the deep intent of Revelation, and this is a point of paramount importance.

But what should be thought of Averroes' concept of the resurrection of the body? We have seen that he professes a certain pragmatism in this regard. The Law in general, and the teaching of the resurrection of bodies in particular, are useful for keeping order in the community, and for the happiness of the individual in this world. But is there a reality behind the colorfully painted pictures of the Paradise and Gehenna reserved for the common man? After all, that is what matters to the ordinary believer. It is certain that the most elementary reasonable reflection could not support such representations, and that Averroes could not add his faith to them. Nevertheless, they do not boil down to a simple lure to draw obedience, or to a simple scarecrow to turn away disobedience to the Law. We can allow that Averroes believed in the resurrection of the body with a reasonable faith, although he could not prove it. The philosophers [who follow Aristotle], he said, "think that there is no life in this world for the man without practical sciences, and that there is no life for him in either this world or the world hereafter without the speculative virtues. Practical sciences and speculative virtues, according to them, do not reach their final state and their perfection except through moral virtues" (*Tahāfut*, p. 582, 3). It is the Aristotelian theory: speculative virtues, in man, cannot go without moral virtues, and moral virtues are tied to activities that bring the body and the soul into the picture. Moral virtue, Averroes notes, "is perfect only through the knowledge of God and the acts of worship that the Law commands." These acts are the gestures and rites in which the body takes part, like it takes part in the observance of all the commandments. Consequently, since the moral virtues, which involve the body, are indispensable in this world for contemplative virtues, such will also be true in the next life, where contemplation will not be purely spiritual, but will still need the assistance of the moral virtues which involve a relationship to the body. Moreover, since the soul is an inseparable unity and since some of its faculties use the body's organs as instruments, it is conceivable that the immortal soul will remain that of a body, not an immortal body, but one resurrected for the soul's needs.

On the resurrection itself, Averroes follows the Qurʾān. It is clear that it will not be the cadavers that take life back and come out of their tombs. From the Qurʾānic perspective, the resurrection is a second creation. The soul could actually be the soul of any body, and we have seen that Averroes, like all Muslims, rejects metempsychosis. This is why resurrected bodies will be bodies resembling (*amthāl*) those that lived on the earth. We can thus conclude that Averroes somewhat wisely decided not to apply demonstrative reasoning to these essentially religious questions. He likewise rejected the dialectical arguments of the theologians who proffered only appearances, often verbal; but relying on what he knew that was proven and certain, he attempted to show the possibility of admitting the religious beliefs of Islam, and to give them a meaning that could be received by reason.

Was Averroes a religious spirit? If what we understand by the question is that in his view religion has a reality and an importance that cannot be passed over in silence, the answer is yes, not only because of his pragmatic interest, but also because it opens the way to the philosopher's reflection on objects that pure reason cannot reach, which are obscure in themselves, but which raise questions for man that he cannot escape. Consequently, if everything that is knowable by demonstration falls under the domain of philosophy, philosophy cannot claim to have the ability to know everything by rational proofs. But it knows the limits of its power. And if the philosopher wanders beyond these limits, he is not unaware of the fact that he can apprehend only possibilities, not certitudes. Such is the condition of man. This being made clear, Averroes does not appear to have had tremendous religious sensitivity, if we judge by his rejection of mysticism. Whatever the case, nothing allows us to doubt that he was a sincere believer.

Chronology

1062–1106: Emirate of Yūsuf ibn Tāshfīn, who founded Marrakesh and created the Almoravid Empire with the conquest of Morocco (1063–1082).

1106–1142: Reign of ʿAlī ibn Yūsuf, who consolidated the union between Morocco and Spain.

1125: Beginnings of the Almohad revolt in the Atlas.

1126: Birth of Averroes.

1147: Victory of the Almohads and fall of Marrakesh. The Almohad dynasty lasted until 1269.

1153: Averroes is in Marrakesh.

1163–1184: Caliphate of Abū Yaʿqūb Yūsuf.

1169: Averroes is cadi in Seville.

1171: Averroes is cadi in Cordoba.

1182: Averroes replaces Ibn Tufayl as first physician to Abū Yaʿqūb Yūsuf.

1184–1199: Caliphate of Abū Yūsuf Yaʿqūb al-Mansūr. Averroes remains in favor.

1195–1197: Averroes falls into disgrace and is banished to Lucena, near Cordoba.

1198: Back in favor, Averroes dies in Marrakesh, where he is buried. Later his body is returned to Cordoba.

1199: Averroes' funeral in Cordoba, attended by the great mystic Muhyī 'l-Dīn al-ʿArabī, who was still quite young.

Glossary

[Transcriptions of the Arabic words below do not carry the diacritical markings that distinguish letters of the Arabic alphabet not present in the Roman alphabet. Readers familiar with Arabic should be able to reconstruct them.]

ʿādāʾ.   Habit. According to Ashʿarite theologians, the existence and the constancy of the cause and effect relationship is assured by a habit of God. A synonym in this sense is *sunna*, custom, whence the *Sunna*, the collection of the *hadiths* or words and deeds of Muhammad.

ʿadl.   Justice. A Qurʾānic term (cf. Qurʾān 4:58: When you pass judgment among men, pass it with justice!).

aḥkām.   The five juridical categories: that which is prescribed, that which is forbidden, that which is suggested, that which is discouraged, and that which is allowed.

al-ākhira.   The Life Hereafter, life after the resurrection, in Heaven or Hell.

ʿālam.   The world. The Qurʾān uses this word in the plural: *ʿālamīn*.

ʿalāqa.   Attachment, affection. A word used by Averroes in conjunction with "love" to characterize the union of the soul and the body.

ʿamal.   Action, operation. *ʿAmalī*: practical, as opposed to *naẓarī*, theoretical.

amr.   The Divine Commandment. A Qurʾānic word which denotes the commandment from both the moral and legisla-

	tive points of view and, at the same time, from the point of view of the laws that govern the world (cf. Qurʾān 7:54, "Is it not to Him (God) that the power to create and commandment belong? Blessed be God, the Master of the Worlds!").
ʿaql.	The intellect. A philosophical term not found in the Qurʾān, although the verb with the same root does appear, meaning "to understand." *Al-maʿqūlāt:* objects of intellect. *Al-ʿaql al-hayūlānī:* the material intellect. *Al-ʿaql al-faʿʿāl:* the active intellect. *Al-ʿaql biʾl-malaka:* the intellect *in habitu. Al-ʿaql al-mustafād:* acquired intellect.
ʿarad.	Accident (philosophical term).
āya, pl. āyāt.	Sign. A Qurʾānic word meaning, on the one hand, the marks that justify the Prophet's mission, and on the other, the proofs of the existence of God and of His attributes discernible in the order of creation. Averroes is interested only in the latter meaning.
ʿawīs.	Obscure, difficult to understand, indecipherable, unsolvable.
azal.	Eternity, preexistence; *azalī:* eternal. A non-Qurʾānic word, often used for eternity *a parte ante*. In this sense, the word is synonymous with *qidam;* from this root, the adjective *qadīm* is Qurʾānic, with the meaning of "old" or "ancient." The difference between eternity in the past and eternity in the future is marked by the expressions *mā lam yazal wa lā yazālu*, "what has not ceased and what will not cease," phrases taken from the Qurʾān (e.g., 13:31): "The infidels will not cease (*lā yazālu*) to be touched by unhappiness."
badan.	An organic body; a human body. Cf. *jism:* body, in general; *jirm*, pl. *ajrām:* corporal mass; this word is used to denote celestial bodies (*al-ajrām al-samāwiyya*, or *al-falakiya*).
bayyin.	Clear, evident. *Bayān:* explanation, proof. *Tabyīn:* explication.
bidʿa.	Blamable innovation in the matter of dogma or law.

dalīl.	Indication, or direction sign, whence indicative proof. A Qurʾānic word (cf. 25:45: "We have made of the sun an indication of darkness"). From the same root as *istidlāl:* induction.
dawr.	Circle, tour, rotation (whence the word *douar,* a small administrative district).
dhāt.	Essence, the opposite of accidents (*aʿrād*).
dhimmi.	A Jewish, Christian, Sabean, or Zoroastrian subject in a Muslim State. These are the "People of the Book" (*Ahl al-Kitāb*) who, having received a revelation, are not forced to choose between death and conversion to Islam when their country is conquered and occupied during a holy war, but who can hold onto their beliefs, their religious practices, and their Law, provided they do so without exterior manifestations and under the condition that they submit to Muslim authority for everything else. In this sense, their lives and their goods are, in principle, protected; the word *dhimma* means "protection." As *dhimmis,* they must nevertheless pay a tax called *jizya.*
didd.	Opposite. A term from the field of logic different from "contradictory" (*munāqid*).
dīn.	Religion in general, although limited in the Qurʾān to the religion of the Muslims and that of the People of the Book, despite the errors that deform the latter (cf. Qurʾān 4:171 "Oh People of the Book! Do not step beyond the bounds of your religion"). But "in the eyes of God, Islam is religion" (3:19). Cf. *milla.* Just as the believer, *muʾmin,* is a Muslim.
duniā.	The world here below; this world. *Al-hayāt al-duniā:* life in this world. Opposite of the Life Hereafter (*al-ākhira*).
falak (pl. aflāq).	The celestial sphere. *Falak al-tadwīr:* orbit of a celestial body (cf. *dawr*). *Al-falakī:* astronomer; *ʿilm al-falak:* astronomy.

falsafa.	Philosophy. *Faylasūf*, pl. *falāsifa*: philosopher.
farḍ.	An obligatory prescription. *Farḍ ʿayn:* a prescription imposed upon each believer personally; *farḍ kifāya:* a prescription imposed on the community as a whole; it suffices that it be observed that a few faithful are fulfilling their duty (as in the case of the obligation to a holy war; believers do not all have to go into combat, but *jihād* is a duty for the community).
fayḍ.	Emanation. A technical word by which Neoplatonists and the Eastern *falāsifa* attempted to explain the birth of the plurality of beings coming from the One, using the image of light radiating from the sun. The Arabic root actually evokes the flowing over of something too full of water (cf. Qurʾān 7:50): "The people of Hell will call this out to the people of paradise: Let water flow over (*afīdū*) upon us."
fiʿl (pl. afʿāl).	Actuality, as opposed to potentiality (*quwwa*). *Biʾl-fiʿl:* in actuality.
fikr.	Reflective thought, reflection. The verbal root is from the Qurʾān, in the sense of reflecting. (Cf. Qurʾān 2:219 and 266): "Thus does God explain the signs to you. Perhaps you will reflect."
fiqh.	Law, jurisprudence. *Al-faqīh*, pl. *al-fuqahāʾ*: jurist, jurisconsultant.
furūʿ (plural of farʿ).	The branches of law, in contrast to the principles of law (*uṣūl al-fiqh*).
gharaḍ.	Goal. Synonym of *hadaf*: design, objective.
ghurnūq (pl. gharānīq).	1. Crane (the bird). 2. Young man with a beautiful face; a woman of great beauty. In the satanic verses, the goddesses of Mecca are called by this name.
ḥadd.	1. Logical definition by the next genus and specific difference, in contrast to *rasm*, descriptive definition. 2. Pl. *ḥudūd* [*Allāh*], a Qurʾānic term of penal law: legal punishment defined literally in the Law, e.g. Qurʾān 24:2: "The adulterous man and the adulterous woman, whip each one hundred times with a whip."

Glossary

ḥadīth. Traditions of the Prophet Muhammad, collected in the *Sunna*.

ḥādith. That which comes in time. *Ḥudūth:* "adventitiousness," contingency.

ḥajj. The pilgrimage to Mecca, or the great pilgrimage, in contrast to the ʿ*umra*, or lesser pilgrimage, which can be made at any time of the year.

ḥakīm. A wise person. *Ḥikma:* wisdom, sagacity; sometimes philosophy. *Ḥākim:* a magistrate, a judge. *Ḥakam:* arbitrator. *Ḥukm:* authority, juridical decision, sentence.

ḥaqq. 1. Law: *al-ḥaqq al-ilāhī* (cf. pl. *ḥuqūq Allāh*), divine law (the laws of God), that is, man's duties toward Him; *al-ḥaqq al-adamī*, human law, that is, the duties of men toward one another, imposed by the Law. 2. Real. *Al-ḥaqīqa:* reality.

hayūlā. Prime matter, as distinct from *al-madda*, the second matter. This distinction is not always respected.

ḥiss. Sense, sensation. *iḥsās:* the act of sensing.

hudā. Direction, straight path, guide of conduct. The Qurʾān presents itself as a *hudā* for believers.

huwiyya. Ipseity. An abstract term drawn from the pronoun *huwa*, he, him; Latin, *ipse*.

iḍāfa. The category of relation. Cf. *al-nisba:* relationship.

ijmāʿ. Community consensus; a principle of law. This idea, inapplicable (given the fact that there was no organism instituted to put it into practice), has been reduced to the consensus of the doctors of the great cities in the Islamic world, or to the consensus of the Companions of the Prophet (by the Ẓāhirite Ibn Ḥazm of Cordoba). In actuality, consensus has often been tacit.

ijtihād. Personal effort to understand the religious texts and the traditions. It is recommended, even obligatory in the exercise of certain functions, such as the function of the caliph who should be capable of it in order to be entrusted with his duties. It stands in contrast to *taqlīd*, blind imitation. And the *mujtahid* who makes this effort, stands in contrast

	to the *muqallid*, who does not. The word comes from the same root as *jihād*, "holy war."
ikhtilāf.	Divergence of opinion in questions of religion. It is considered to be the greatest of evils. Knowledge of divergences is a science related to the science of law and theology in Islam.
ikhtiyār.	Free choice; whence, free will.
ilah (pl. āliha).	Divinity, god (common name). Allāh is the proper name of God. Cf. the statement of faith: *lā ilah illa 'llāh:* "There is no divinity but God."
ᶜilla.	Cause. In particular, it denotes one of Aristotle's four causes (efficient, material, formal, and final). *Sabab* means cause in the sense of "reason," or "motive."
ᶜilm.	Science, knowledge. The word *maᶜrifa* (knowledge) often has the meaning of "gnosis."
imkān.	Possibility. *Mumkin:* possible.
intiqāl.	Passage from one state to another.
irāda.	Will, in general; the will of God differentiated, as a will toward benevolence, from *mashīʾa:* absolute will of decree. Cf. the expression *In shāʾa'Llāh:* "If God wills."
istiᶜdād.	Disposition.
istikmāl.	Perfect accomplishment. In philosophy: entelechy, the being in actuality in its perfection.
istimrār.	Constancy, perseverance in a state.
istinbāṭ.	Invention. In logic, deduction. Cf. *istidlāl:* induction.
iṭlāq (ᶜalā'l-iṭlāq or bi'l-iṭlāq).	Absolutely. *Mulaq:* absolute, unconditional.
ittiḥād.	Union with God, for mystics; it was rejected by speculative theologians as impossible, because of divine transcendence.
ittiṣāl.	Conjunction with God, for mystics who do not go so far as to admit union. For Avempace, conjunction of the human intellect with the active intellect, resulting in the happiness of the Blessed.

jamāʿa.	Collectivity. This is not a Qurʾānic word. In the Qurʾān, the word *umma* is found to refer to the community of the Prophet. The *jamāʿa* can then be considered as the collectivity of believers united by common faith in the face of innovators and heretics, while the *umma* is the juridical and religious community founded on the Law and the sociopolitical organization of the Muslims. Thus, in contrast to the Shiʿites (*al-shīʿa*), the Sunnis took the name *ahl al-sunna wa'l-jamāʿa* (people of Tradition, members of the orthodox community). Nevertheless, the two expressions are often interchanged.
jawhar.	Precious stone, jewel. In philosophy, it has taken on the meaning of "substance."
jirm (pl. ajrām).	Body. This word, which is lexically a synonym of *jism*, was used by the astronomers to refer to celestial bodies which, according to Aristotle, are simple and formed of a fifth element, the quintessence.
jism.	The body in general. The adjective *jismī* refers to what is of the body, as opposed to that which is incorporeal. The philosophers and the Muʿtazilites argued to know whether it was infinitely divisible. The Ashʿarites adopted an atomic theory.
kalām.	1. Language, word, discourse. 2. Speculative theology. *Al-mutakallim:* the theologian (pl. *al-mutakallimūn*).
kalīma.	Word. The word was used by translators for the Greek *logos* in all its meanings.
kawn.	The fact of being one thing or another. The verb *kāna* means the manner of being, rather than the simple fact of being. Whence, *al-mutakawwin:* that which becomes one being or another; *al-kaynūna:* the mode of being, whence existence, understood as one existence or another.
khalīfa.	The caliph, the successor to the Prophet as head of the Islamic community, whence his title of Commander of the Believers (*amīr al-muʾminīn*). In principle, he is named in a selection process by the

important members of the community, the number of electors varying and ultimately becoming only one, since the ruling caliph proposed his successor to the homage (*bayʿa*) of the community, which soon became tacit, such that the Sunni caliphate ended up being hereditary, for all practical purposes. When there were two caliphs, one in Iraq and the other in Spain, the Almoravids, since they recognized the sovereignty of the Abbasids in Baghdad, took the title *Amīr al-muslimīn* (Commander of the Muslims). But the Almohads took back the title of Commander of Believers. The Imamate of the Shiʿites was hereditary in the Prophet's family, due to a Qurʾānic text (33:33) on the People of the House (*Ahl al-bayt*), corroborated by a tradition that applies to the People of the Cloak (*Ahl al-kissāʾ*): ʿAlī, Fātima and their two sons, Ḥasan and Ḥusayn.

khāliq. The Creator: God.

khayāl (al-). Imagination. *Al-suwar al-khayāliyya:* the forms of the imagination.

kufr. Infidelity, unbelief. *Al-kāfir:* the infidel. *Takfīr:* accusation of infidelity, bringing with it condemnation to death. For this reason, the doctors of the law generally avoid encouraging the pronouncement of such a serious sentence.

kull (al-). All; the Universe. *Al-kulliyyāt:* the universals, a term from logic. *Al-Kulliyyāt fī'l-Ṭibb* ("The Generalities of Medicine"), one of Averroes' works, the Latin *Colliget*.

kunnāsh (pl. kanānīsh). A general treatise on medical therapy.

lāḥiq (pl. lawāḥiq). Concomitant (concomitants).

lāzim (pl. lawāzim). That which follows (those which follow).

lawlab. Spiral, helix. *Al-ḥarakat al-lawlabiyya:* movement in a spiral; helicoidal movement.

Glossary

maʿād.	A Qurʾānic word meaning the place to which one returns: "He who prescribed the Qurʾān to you is He Who brings you back to the place of return" (28:85). Whence, the implicit meaning, "future life."
maʿnā.	The meaning of what one is trying to say. Whence, the signification in philosophy, of "meaningful intent," and, in general, "everything that carries meaning." The word eludes easy translation, and in some ways is a "catch all" that is occasionally translated simply as "a something."
madīna.	City, whence the adjective *madanī:* political.
madhhab.	1. Religious doctrine. 2. School of law, a word that refers, in particular, to the four official schools of law: Mālikī, Shāfiʿī, Hanbalī, and Hanafī.
maḥabba.	Love. A Qurʾānic word (20:39) used in Averroes' texts in the general sense of attachment (of the soul to its body).
māhiyya.	Quiddity. A technical word coined and formed from the pronoun *mā* (what), just as *quiddity* is derived from the Latin *quid*.
malaka.	*Habitus.* Since Arabic does not have the verb "have," like Latin and Greek, the Arabs coined an equivalent of *habitus* from the verb *malaka*, meaning "to possess."
manqūl.	An argument that is based on a tradition, as opposed to one based on reason (*maʿqūl*).
matn.	The textual contents of a tradition that follow the string of names of the tradition's successive reporters, the *isnād*, or "chain of support."
mawāʿiẓ (sing. mawʿiẓa).	Exhortations, preaching.
mawḍūʿ.	Object (philosophical term).
mawjūd.	The existing being (literally: what is found). *Al-wujūd:* existence.
miḥna.	Trial. The name given to the inquisitory procedure carried out against non-Muʿtazilites following the official adoption of Muʿtazilism by the caliph al-Maʾmūn,

	for the purpose of imposing the teaching of a created Qurʾān. The majority of doctors believe that the Qurʾān is the letter of the eternal Word of God.
milla.	Religious confession. The Qurʾān speaks of Abraham's confession (*millat Ibrāhīm,* 2:130) as the pure and true religion; in this sense, Abraham can already be called a Muslim (*muslim,* 3:67).
mithāl.	Type, model. In the plural (*muthul*), the word refers to Platonic ideas among the philosophers.
muʿālaja.	Medical treatment.
mudawwana.	The code. *Al-Mudawwana al-kubrā,* title of the work by the great Malikī doctor from Kairouan, Sahnūn (d. 240/854).
muhsanāt.	In the Qurʾān, this word refers to chaste women, "ladies," in the medieval sense of the word: "Those who accuse ladies without being able to produce four witnesses, give them 80 lashes with a whip" (24:4).
murajjiḥ.	That which tips the plate on a scale. The reason for a decision, the motive that forces an action.
munāsaba.	Relationship implying agreement, proportion, or convenience. From the same root, *nisba:* relationship (in the general sense of the word).
muqaddama or muqaddima.	1. Premise. A term from logic; premises of a syllogism. 2. Introduction (to a work).
muqāyasa.	Putting something into parallel; analogy by comparison.
muzāwala.	Practice of a science or an art. Practicum.
nafs (pl. nufūs anfus).	The soul. *Al-ṣuwar al-nafsāniyya:* the psychic forms.
naghama.	Melody; melodic harmony.
najm (pl. nujūm), or najma.	Star, from the verb *najama:* to appear, to rise, to come out (as a star).
nāmūs.	Law; taken from the Greek *nomos. Nāmūs ṭabīʿī; nāmūs adabī:* natural law and moral law (these

ideas are purely Greek; in Islam, all laws are positive laws, instituted by God). *Nawāmīs al-ṭabīʿa:* the laws of nature.

naskh. Abrogation. Abrogation is an important principle of juridical exegesis of the Qurʾān, which is based on verse 2:106: "We do not abrogate or throw into oblivion a verse without revealing a similar one, or a better one." The exegetes wondered how one revealed verse could be better than another. They ultimately decided that it was better for the people to whom it was addressed. Thus, the Mosaic Law, which was good for the Jews, was abrogated by the Laws that Jesus brought, which were better for Christians, but which were abrogated by Muhammad's law, the best for all men, and which will thus not be abrogated. It has been argued whether one Qurʾānic verse can abrogate another, and consequently whether abrogation can take place within a Law itself. This has been seen as impossible by some doctors. Nevertheless, there are Qurʾānic verses that exclude one another, and this situation is almost impossible to bring into harmony. If we bring abrogation in to preserve coherence, we are thus forced to admit that Qurʾānic revelation, which took place over a period of ten years, took into consideration the inevitable evolution of the Prophet's teaching, depending on the circumstances in which he found himself. Whatever the case, Averroes generally thought that "the best is abrogated by what is better than it" (*al-afḍal yunsakhu bimā afḍal minhu* in *Tahāfut*, B, p. 583).

naẓar. 1. Look, vision. 2. Speculation. *Naẓarī:* speculative, theoretical; opposite of *ʿamalī:* practical.

nuṭq. Articulated language; word. *Nāṭiq:* endowed with word, with reason. *Al-insān ḥayawān nāṭiq:* man is a reasonable animal.

qadhf. A calumnious accusation. Not a Qurʾānic word.

qānūn. Rule, canon. The word is from Greek. *Al-Qānūn fī'l-Ṭibb:* "The Canon of Medicine," one of Avicenna's works.

qisṭās. Scale. A Qurʾānic word (17:35 and 26:182): "Weigh with an accurate scale" (*bi'l-qisṭās al-mustaqīm*), whence the title of a work by Ghazālī.

qiyās.	Etymologically, this word, which refers to reasoning based on comparison or analogy (*qāsa*: to measure, to compare), was selected by Arab logicians to denote the syllogism.
qudra.	Qurʾānic word for divine power.
quwwa.	Force, strength. In philosophy, it refers to potentiality as opposed to actuality. *Bi'l-quwwa:* in potentiality. The Qurʾān uses the word once in the sense of *qudra*, in reference to God (52:58): "God possesses unshakable force" (*al-quwwat al-matīn*).
rajāʾ.	Hope founded on the promise (*waʿd*) of the reward of Paradise. A Qurʾānic word opposed to *khawf*, the fear founded on the threat (*waʿīd*) of the punishments of Hell.
rasd.	Observation. *Rasd al-kawākib, rasd al-aflāk:* observation of the heavenly bodies. *Marsad:* observatory.
raʾy.	Personal point of view, allowed as a principle of law by some (Hanafī) schools, but rejected by others. The Prophet is said to have left to some emissaries the freedom to judge according to their personal points of view, when they were far from him and had neither texts nor instructions. The opponents of *raʾy*, on the other hand, thought that this circumstantial permission could not be raised to the status of a principle.
rūḥ.	Spirit, a Qurʾānic term. *Rūḥānī:* coming from the spirit, spiritual. *Al-ṣuwar al-rūḥāniyya:* spiritual forms.
sabab.	Cause, motive (cf. *ʿilla*).
ṣaḥīḥ.	Of good merit, authentic. Refers to the traditions in which one can have absolute confidence. Cf. *ṣiḥḥa:* authenticity, validity, truth.
samāʾ.	Sky. *Samāwī:* celestial, of the sky.
sharīʿa.	The Qurʾānic Law that governs the Islamic community. *Al-sharʿ:* the Law as revelation. *Ṣāḥib al-sharīʿa:* legislator.
shayʾ (pl. ashyāʾ).	Thing. The word is common in the Qurʾān, with the very general sense of that which exists: "God is powerful

	over all things" (2:20, for example). Avicenna used it, along with the relative "what" (*mā*), to express Aristotle's term for being as being, since if one wishes to define a being, one must say: "it is the thing that," or "it is what . . . ."
shūrā.	Consultation, a principle of goverment in the community. Cf. Qurʾān 42:38: "Those whose affairs are regulated by consultation with one another."
ṣinʿa.	Art created by an artisian; it is often taken as the equivalent of "science." For example, *ṣinaʿat al-ṭibb,* the art of medicine. *Al-ṣāniʿ:* artisan, worker. The Qurʾān speaks of the work of God (*ṣunʿ Allāh,* 27:88). But He is its Creator (*khāliq*) and not the artisan (*ṣāniʿ*).
ṣinf (pl. aṣnāf).	Sort, or kind. It refers to individuals all marked by the same quality, although not in the formal, logical sense, where "species" might be used.
suʿadāʾ (sing. saʿīd).	Happy, blessed. *Saʿāda:* happiness, beatitude.
Ṣūra (pl. ṣuwar).	Form, as opposed to matter. *Al-ṣuwar al-taʿlīmiyya,* mathematical forms.
ṭabīʿa.	Nature (root *ṭabaʿa*: to print). The idea here is that of an impression; cf. Greek: *sphragis.*
taʿallum.	Apprenticeship, learning (the fact of acquiring knowledge).
taʾwīl.	Commentary in the figurative sense (*majāz*), allegorical exegesis. In-depth but nonliteral understanding of a text, as opposed to *tafsīr:* simple explanatory commentary.
taghayyur.	Alteration (cf. *ghayr:* other than), change, transformation.
tajriba.	Trial, whence experiment, experimentation.
takdhīb.	Accusation of lying or of error. Whence, a negative judgment.
taqlīd.	Imitation, blind acceptance of a teaching. *Al-muqallid:* he who blindly follows a teaching; as opposed to *mujtahid*.

taṣawwur.	Representation, conception (the first operation of the mind), concept.
taṣdīq.	Judgment of veracity (*ṣidq*), positive judgment; judgment in general: the second operation of the spirit.
tawḥīd.	Confession of the unicity of God. A fundamental teaching of the Qurʾān. Whence: monotheistic theology.
ṭibb.	Medicine. *Al-ṭabīb:* doctor. The word has passed in the French language as a slang word for "physician": *toubib.*
ṭūr.	A manner of being; mode of being.
ukra (pl. ukar).	Globe.
umma.	The universal Muslim community. *Ummat al-Nabī:* the community of the Prophet.
uṣūl (sing. aṣl).	Principle. *Uṣūl al-fiqh, al-dīn:* principles of law, of religion. Opposite of *furūʿ* (sing. *farʿ*): the derived branches.
wāhib.	Giver, donor. *Wāhib al-ṣuwar:* the giver of forms (*dator formarum*); the separate active intellect, the angel Gabriel, for the Eastern *falāsifa.*
wājib.	Necessary. *Wājib al-wujūd:* the being whose existence is necessary, the necessary Being, God, for Avicenna. N.B. A distinction should be made between the *ḍarūrī* (the compeller)—which includes the necessary (*wājib*) and the impossible (*mumtaniʿ*), which forces one another into thought—and the possible (*mumkin*), which leaves a choice.
waqt.	The moment, the instant.
wujūd.	Existence. Cf. *al-mawjūd* (pl. *al-mawjūdāt*): existing being(s).
yābis.	Dryness. One of the four elementary qualities. The others are *al-ruṭūba:* humidity; *al-ḥarāra:* heat; and *al-burūda:* cold.
yaqīn.	Certitude.

yamīn (pl. aymān).	Oath.
ẓāhir.	That which is apparent or manifest; the manifest sense of a word or phrase. Opposite of *bāṭin:* what is hidden. Ẓāhirism is the teaching that takes texts in their apparent sense. These words are applied to God: "He is the First and the Last, the Manifest and the Hidden" (Qurʾān 57:3).
zaman.	Continuous time.
ẓann.	Opinion; it corresponds to the Greek *doxa*.

Bibliography

ALLARD, M.
"Le rationalisme d'Averroès d'après une étude sur la création." *Bulletin des Études orientales,* XIV, 1952–1954.

ALONSO, M.
"Averroes observador de la naturaleza." *Al-Andalus,* V, 1940.
"El 'ta'wil' Y la hermeneutica sacra de Averroes." *Al-Andalus,* VII, 1942.

ARNALDEZ, R.
"La pensée religieuse d'Averroès." In *Aspects de la pensée musulmane.* Vrin-Reprise, n.d., pp. 251–300.

CHRIST, P. S.
The Psychology of the Active Intellect of Averroes. Philadelphia, 1926.

CRUZ HERNANDEZ, M.
"La libertad y la naturaleza social del hombre según Averroes." In *L'Homme et son destin.* Louvain, 1960.
"Etica e Politica na Filosofia de Averrois." In *Revue portugaise de Philosophie, XVII,* 1961.

DAVIDSON, H. A.
Alfarabi, Avicenna, and Averroes on Intellect: Their Cosmologies, Theories of the Active Intellect, and Theories of Human Intellect. New York: Oxford University Press, 1992.

DE BOER, T. J.
Die Widersprüche der Philosophie und ihr Ausgleich durch Ibn Roschd. Strasbourg, 1894.

GAUTHIER, L.
La théorie d'Ibn Roschd sur les rapports de la religion et de la philosophie. Paris, 1909.

HORTEN, M.
Die Metaphysik des Averroës. Halle, 1912.
Die Hauptlehren des Averroes nach seiner Schrift: die Widerlegung des Gazali. Bonn, 1913.

DE LIBERA, A., AND M. R. HAYOUN
Averroès et l'averroisme. Paris, PUF (Que sais-je).
Averroès et la question du sujet. Paris, Aubier.

MEHREN, F.
"Études sur la philosophie d'Averroès concernant ses rapports avec celle d'Avicenne et de Gazzali." *Muséon,* VII, 1888–89.

NALLINO, C. A.
"Averroès" in *Enciclopedia italiana* (article, n.d.).

URVOY, D.
Ibn Rushd (Averroes). Trans. O. Stewart. London, New York: Routledge, 1991.
Les ambitions d'un intellectuel musulman. Paris: Flammarion, 1998.

Annotated Index of Proper Names

[Transcriptions of the Arabic words below do not carry the diacritical markings that distinguish letters of the Arabic alphabet not present in the Roman alphabet. Readers familiar with Arabic should be able to reconstruct them. For Muslims, the first date given is that of the Hegira (hijra), and the second is the corresponding date from the Gregorian calendar.]

ʿAbd al-Wāḥid al-Marrākushī *(581/1185–date of death unknown)*
A chronicler from Marrakesh. He spent some time in Cordoba, then in Seville, before undertaking a trip to the East in 613/1217. In 621/1224, while in Baghdad, he composed his *Histoire des Almohades* (translated into French by Fagnan, Albiers, 1893).

Abū Bakr ibn al-ʿArabī (468/1076–543/1148)
Traditionist from Seville. Author of a number of works, many of which are no longer extant; we do have his juridical commentary on the Qurʾān, *Aḥkām al-Qurʾān*, 5 vols. in octavo, Arabic text, Cairo 1376/1957.

Abū Jaʿfar ibn Hārūn al-Ṭarjālī (from Trujillo, in Estremadura)
Physician from a notable family of Seville, famous for his method and the quality of his treatments. He was especially competent in treating diseases of the eyes (*ṣināʿat al-kuhl*), and it is said that "with the help of God" he healed a child who had a wood splinter stuck in his pupil. He was also a philosopher who knew the books of Aristotle and other "sages" of Antiquity, and he was versed in the science of *hadith*. He was in the service of the Almohad caliph Abū Yaʿqūb Yūsuf, the father of Yaʿqūb al-Manṣūr. In his legal studies he was the student of Abū Bakr ibn al-ʿArabī, to whom he was attached for a long time. He was one of Averroes' teachers in the field of medicine.

Abū Marwān ibn Zuhr (Abhomeron Avenzoar)
   Born in Seville, where he also died (circa 484/1092–557/1161). He was a friend of Averroes and the author of a number of works, including *Taysir fi'l-mudāwāt wa'l-tadbīr* ("Practical Manual of Treatments and Diets"), *Kitāb al-aghdhya* ("Book of Foods"), and *Kitāb al-iqtisād fī islāh al-anfus wa'l-ājsād* ("Book on Balance in the Refection of Souls and Bodies"). Abū Marwān was primarily an observer. Of special note is his description of mediastinal tumors: *al-awrām allatī tahdathu fī'l-ghishā' alladhī yaqsimu al-sadr tūlan* (tumors produced in the membrane that separates the length of the chest), and also his observation of pericardial absesses: *awrām fī ghishā' al-kalb* (tumors of the membrane of the heart).

Abū Yaʿqūb Yūsuf (d. 580/1184)
   Second sovereign of the Almohad dynasty, who ruled from 558/1163 to 580/1184. He surrounded himself with famous philosophers, physicians, and poets.

Aflatūn
   Arabic name for Plato.

ʿAlī ibn Yūsuf ibn Tāshufīn
   Almoravid emir who reigned over a large part of the Maghreb and southern Spain from 500/1106 to 537/1143. He died in 537/1143, five years before Marrakesh was taken by ʿAbd al-Muʾmin ibn ʿAlī, successor to Mahdī Ibn Tūmart, who inspired the Almohad movement.

ʿAlī Rabbān al-Ṭabarī
   Physician from Tabaristān, in Asia; he was the son of the famous astronomer and mathematician Sahl Rabbān al-Ṭabarī, who taught him medicine, geometry, and philosophy, as well as a number of languages: Arabic, Syriac, perhaps also Hebrew and some Greek. What he wrote about his father who, because of his knowledge and his piety, was nicknamed Rabbān (an honorary title given to doctors of the Sanhedrin), suggests that his family was Jewish. He converted to Islam when he became secretary to the prince of Tabaristān and was a highly visible individual in the court of the caliphs al-Muʿtasim and al-Mutawakkil. His primary work was a *kunnāsh* entitled *Firdaws al-hikma* ("The Paradise of Wisdom"), where he cites Hippocrates, Galen, Dioscoridus, as well as Indian works, the *Charaka Samhita* and the *Susruta Samhita*. He was the teacher of Muḥammad ibn Zakariyya al-Rāzī, the famous physician known in Latin as Razes.

Aristūtuālīs (Arisū)
   Arabic name for Aristotle. The totality of his works (beginning with his works on logic) was progressively translated by Christians into Syriac, and

then into Arabic, as were his great Greek commentators, particularly Alexander of Aphrodisus and Themistius, whom Averroes cites.

Ashᶜarī (Abū'l-Ḥasan) (260/873–324/935) and Ashᶜarism
A student of the Muʿtazilites, he broke away from them, while still retaining their style of rational argumentation, which Averroes called dialectic. In opposition to them, he claimed that the Qurʾān was eternal and uncreated. He also believed in the reality of divine attributes; the creation by God of human acts that became man's only by "acquisition" (*kasb*); the negation of the intermediate position of the sinner (*manzila bayn al-manzilatayn*) who, according to the Muʿtazilites, would be neither a believer nor an infidel—the sinner, according to Ashᶜarī, remains a believer, but he will be punished.

Al-Bāqillānī (Abū Bakr Muhammad)
Born in Basra (date unknown), he died in Baghdad in 403/1013. An Ashᶜarite theologian and Mālikī jurist, he was a cadi, professor, writer, and polemicist. He was the author of a work on the incomparability of the Qurʾān (*I ᶜjāz al-Qurʾān*), and of a treatise on *Kalām*, the *Tamhīd* ("The Sorting"), in which he outlined his theological concepts as a Muslim and his criticism of religions other than Islam. Several of his works have been left to us incomplete. An introduction to atomism in Islam has been attributed to him, but the present day tendency is to downplay his personal contribution in this regard. His *Tamhīd* is also a representative work about the doctrine.

Al-Bitrūjī (Alpetragius)
A Spanish Arab astronomer, follower and friend of Ibn Ṭufayl. Along with Avempace and Jābir ibn Aflaḥ, he was one of the originators of the return to Aristotle, with the abandonment of epicycles and eccentrics. He believed that the celestial spheres turned around different axes and produced a spiral movement (*ḥaraka lawlabiyya*). He was the author of a *Kitāb fī'l-hayʾa* ("Book on the Configuration of the Sky").

Callippus (early 4th century B.C.)
Greek astronomer, disciple of Eudoxus, to whom Averroes referred in his Great Commentary on Book L of the *Metaphysics*.

Dioscoridus (circa 50 B.C.)
In Arabic: Diyusqūridīs. A Greek physician, author of a *Materia Medica* that had considerable influence on Arabic medicine in the study of foods and medicines.

Eudoxus of Cnidus (circa 406–355)
Greek astronomer, mathematician, and philosopher. Founder of the School of Cysique in Asia Minor. He assumed that the planets were carried on homocentric spheres whose movements, by combining with one another, accounted for their apparent movement. Cited by Averroes.

Fārābī (Abū Naṣr al-)
Arabian Muslim philosopher influenced by Neoplatonism. Born in Fārāb in Turkestan, he died at age 80 in Damascus in 339/950. He wrote a work, the *Kitāb al-jamᶜ*, in which he attempted to unify the thought of the two Sages (Plato and Aristotle), by relying on pseudo-Aristotle's *Theology*. Through his metaphysics and the cosmology he founded on the theory of emanation, and with his treatise on the Intellect (*fī'l-ᶜaql*) and his illuminative theory of intellectual knowledge, he was a direct influence on Avicenna's thinking. His politics inspired Avempace. His work in the field of logic, which was probably influenced by the Syriac language logicians, was known and appreciated even in the Muslim West.

Ghazālī (Abū Hāmid), (450/1058–505/1111)
Ashᶜarite theologian and Muslim jurist, named by Niẓām al-Mulk, in 484/1091, as professor in the *madrasa* that he had founded in Baghdad, the Niẓāmiyya. He studied Avicenna's philosophy, which he explained in his *Maqāsid al-falāsifa* ("The Goals of the Philosophers"), and which he critiqued in his *Tahāfut al-falāsifa* ("The Decay of the Philosophers"). The latter work was subsequently demolished by Averroes. Then he abandoned his professorship and left Baghdad with the excuse of making the Pilgrimage: he was perhaps in fear of the Ismaili Assassins, who were responsible for the death of Nizān al-Mulk. Perhaps, also, he had a crisis of faith and doubts, from which he freed himself by engaging in the mystical life (cf. his autobiographical work: *Al-munqidh min al-dalāl*). He was a prolific writer, his corpus including works of law, theology, and especially the *Iḥyāʾ ᶜulūm al-dīn* ("The Renaissance of the Sciences of Religion").

Hūd
One of the "Arabian" prophets, with Sālih and Shuᶜayb, about whom the Qurʾān speaks. He was sent to the tribe of the ᶜAdites.

Ibn ᶜAbbās (ᶜAbd Allāh)
One of the greatest of the first generation of learned Muslims, the founder of Qurʾānic exegesis. He collected a number of traditions by interviewing the Companions of the Prophet. We are indebted to him for

Annotated Index of Proper Names 153

information regarding the interpretation of Qurʾānic verses and questions of religious law. He died in 68/687.

Ibn Bājja (Avempace), (d. 533/1139)
Philosopher and vizir. He was imprisoned, accused of heresy by the Almoravid Ibrāhīm ibn Yūsuf, and freed through the intervention of Averroes' grandfather. He is famous above all for two works:
1. His *Tadbīr al-mutawaḥḥid* ("Diet of the Solitary"), which was influenced by Fārābī who, in *Al-siyāsat al-madaniyya* ("Politics of the City") and *Fuṣūl al-madanī* ("Aphorisms of the Statesman"), made a study of the nature—good or bad—of cities, and recommended against living in a perverse city.
2. His *Risālat ittiṣūl al-ʿaql bi'l-isnān* ("Letter on the Conjunction of the Intellect with Man"), which attracted Averroes' attention, albeit without convincing him.

Ibn Bashkuwāl
A learned Spanish historian and traditionist of Muslim origin ("Son of Pascual"). He was born in Cordoba in 494/1101 and died in 578/1183. In Seville, he was an auditor of Averroes and of Abū Bakr ibn al-ʿArabī. He was important because of the richness and the depth of his knowledge of the cultural history of Muslim Spain.

Ibn Ḥazm of Cordoba (Abū Muḥammad ʿAlī), (384/994–456/1064)
A poet, historian, jurist, philosopher, and theologian of Muslim Spain. His work was both varied and abundant. He was a historian of religions and of sects in his great work entitled *Fiṣal;* a specialist in the methodology of law in his *Kitāb al-iḥkām fī usūl al-aḥkām* ("On the Exactitude Concerning the Principles of Juridical Categories"); a jurist in his eleven-volume work in octavo entitled *Al-muḥallā* ("The Ornate Work"). In the field of law, he was the most illustrious representative of Ẓāhirism, which interprets the Qurʾān according to the "manifest" literal sense, and in this regard he conceived a Ẓāhirite grammar in which he showed himself to be a theoretician of the language and of the psychology of language. He distinguished himself by his methodical and severe critiques of *ḥadīth;* he vigorously opposed the different schools of law, especially the Shāfiʿī and the Mālikī. He made numerous enemies, and the vicissitudes of the politics to which he was subjected embittered him and made his thinking aggressive. He was particularly famous for his *Ṭawq al-ḥamāma* ("The Necklace of the Dove on Love and Lovers"), in which he showed particular interest in sincerity in the expression of feelings, when the obvious sense of what language says by the very power of language is masked by a psychic purpose hidden beneath the words.

Annotated Index of Proper Names

Ibn Sīnā (Avicenna), (370/980 – 428/1037)
He was born near Bukhārā, in Asia, and Persian, in which he composed his "Book of Knowledge" (*Dānishnāma*), was his native language. But his great works were in Arabic. His philosophical thought was in the same line as that of Fārābī, although it had a more encyclopedic character. His books outlined his ideas according to the tripartite division in common usage: logic, physics, and metaphysics. The main ones are *Kitāb al-shifāʾ* ("Book of Healing"), *Kitāb al-najāʾ* ("Book of Health"), *Kitāb al-ishārāt wa'l-tanbīhāt* ("Book of Directives and Remarks"). His father was affiliated with the Ismaili movement, and it is possible that Avicenna, without belonging to the movement, was influenced by him in his tendencies favoring a Neoplatonism which, according to Henry Corbin, is characterized by gnosticism. This question has been discussed at length, especially regarding the nature of "Oriental Philosophy" (*Al-ḥikmat al-mashriqiyya*), of which only the "Logic of the Orientals" (*Manṭiq al-mashriqiyyīn*) has been left to us. In the field of medicine, Avicenna was the author of the "Canon" (*Qānūn fīʾl-ṭibb*) and of "The Medicine Poem" (*Urjūza fīʾl-ṭibb*).

Ibn Ṭufayl (Abū Bakr), known to Latin readers as Abubacer (d. 581/1185)
Physician and philosopher, he was the author of the treatise entitled *Ḥayy ibn Yaqdhān*, the story of a child raised by a gazelle who little by little and all by himself discovers physical, metaphysical, and religious truths that all end up being in accord, naturally, with the teachings of the Qurʾān. Actually, Ibn Ṭufayl tended toward a vision of the world that was close to that of Muslim theology. In contrast to other *falāsifa*, and to Averroes in particular, he did not allow for the action of "second causes" as powers that govern the celestial spheres. God is the Supreme Being and the only efficient cause. Also in contrast to Avempace and Averroes, he allowed that mystical contemplation is superior to philosophical knowledge.

Ibn Tūmart (c. 471/1078 – 524/1130)
A religious reformer, called the *Mahdī* (the Guided [by God] One). His teachings excluded any belief or practice contrary to the rigorous doctrine of Divine Unicity (*tawḥīd*); the movement he founded is thus referred to as the Almohads (Arabic: *al-muwaḥḥidūn*, the "unitarians"). His revolt against the Almoravids in the hope of reestablishing the purity of religious life made him head of an embryonic state that, with the impetus of ʿAbd al-Muʾmin, became the Muʾminid Dynasty of the Almohads.

Ibrāhīm ibn Yūsuf ibn Tāshfīn
Almoravid emir who founded Marrakesh.

Annotated Index of Proper Names 155

Jālīnūs
The Arabic name for Galen. His influence on Muslim thought in both medicine and philosophy was considerable. His works were translated into Arabic and commentaries were often written on them.

Juwaynī (Abū'l-Maʿālī), (419/1028–478/1085)
Ashʿarite theologian known by the name Imām al-Haramayn (Imam of the two holy cities, Mecca and Medina). He left his native city, near Nishapour, where Ashʿarism had been denounced as an innovation, and travelled to Baghdad, then to the Hijaz where he taught in Mecca and Medina. He was concerned with principles of law and sought to define a juridical method based on Ashʿarite theology. His great work *Kitāb al-irshād ilā qawātiʿ al-adilla fī usūl al-iʿtiqād* ("Book Leading to Decisive Proofs Related to the Principles of Belief") stood out for the importance it accorded to rational procedures of demonstration. The book was translated into French by J. D. Luciani (Paris, 1938).

Lisān al-dīn ibn al-Khatīb (713/1313–776/1375)
The greatest of the Muslim historians of Grenada. He was interested in all branches of knowledge: history, poetry, medicine, philosophy, and mysticism; and he was distinguished in his knowledge of Arabo-Muslim culture in Spain such that it was seen at the end of the 7th/13th century.

Marrākushī. See ʿ*Abd al-Wāhid al-Marrākushī*

Miskawayh (320/932–421/1030)
Philosopher and historian, born in Rayy (Iran). Author of a treatise on ethics, *Tahdhīb al-akhlāq wa-tathīr al-aʿrāq* ("On the Correction of Morals and the Purification of Natures"), and of a work on general philosophy, *Al-fawz al-asghar* ("The Little Book of Health").

Qushayrī (Abū'l-Qāsim), (376/986–465/1072)
Theologian and mystic born in Ustuwā (Khorasan), author of the *Risāla* ("Epistle") that includes a presentation of the great masters of Sufism and the list of technical terms from mysticism as well as the definitions that have been given for them. He is also the author of a mystical commentary on the Qurʾān, *Laṭāʾif al-ishārāt* ("The Fine Points of Illusions").

Qustā ibn Lūqā al-Baʿlabakī
A learned Christian translator. He was born in Balbek and died in Armenia, c. 300/912. Trained in medicine, he practiced his art in Baghdad. He knew Greek, Syriac, and Arabic and, in addition to medicine, he was

learned in philosophy, mathematics, astronomy, and music. He was thus able to translate a great diversity of works by authors such as Diophantus, Hero of Alexandria (whose *Mechanics* is extant only in its Arabic translation), as well as others. His numerous personal works deal with all these subjects more or less equally: commentary on Euclid's *Elements,* on Diophantus' algebra, a study on the celestial sphere, on weights and measures, etc.

About the Author

ROGER ARNALDEZ
Born in Paris in 1911.

After Lycée Louis-le-Grand and Khange, he earned his *license* and his *diplome d'études supérieurs* in philosophy and a certificate in general biology.

PROFESSIONAL ACTIVITIES:

1937	Professor at Lycée de Mont-de-Marsan.
1938–39	Professor at the French Lycée in Cairo.
1939–45	Prisoner-of-war in Germany during World War II.
1945–46	Assistant director at the French Lycée in Cairo.
1946–48	Cultural Attaché in the French embassy in Cairo.
1948–50	Professor at the Franco-Egyptian Lycée in Heliopolis.
1950–55	Professor of classical philosophy at the Egyptian University of ʿAin-Shams (Heliopolis).
1955	Doctorate (Docteur-ès-Lettres).
1955–56	Professor at the Faculté des Lettres in Bordeaux (Arabic Language and Civilization); chair of Muslim Law at the Faculté de Droit. These teaching positions lasted until one year after being named to a position in Lyon.
1956–69	Professor of Muslim Philosophy and Civilization at the Faculté des Lettres in Lyon.
1969–80	Professor of philosophy and Islamology at the Université de Paris IV-Sorbonne.

MEMBERSHIP:
Corresponding member of the Academy of Arabic Language in Cairo.
Associate Member of the Royal Academy of Belgium.
Member of the Académie des Sciences Morales et Politiques in France.

B
749
.Z7
A6913
2000

DATE DUE

MR 29 04			